W9-BFP-884

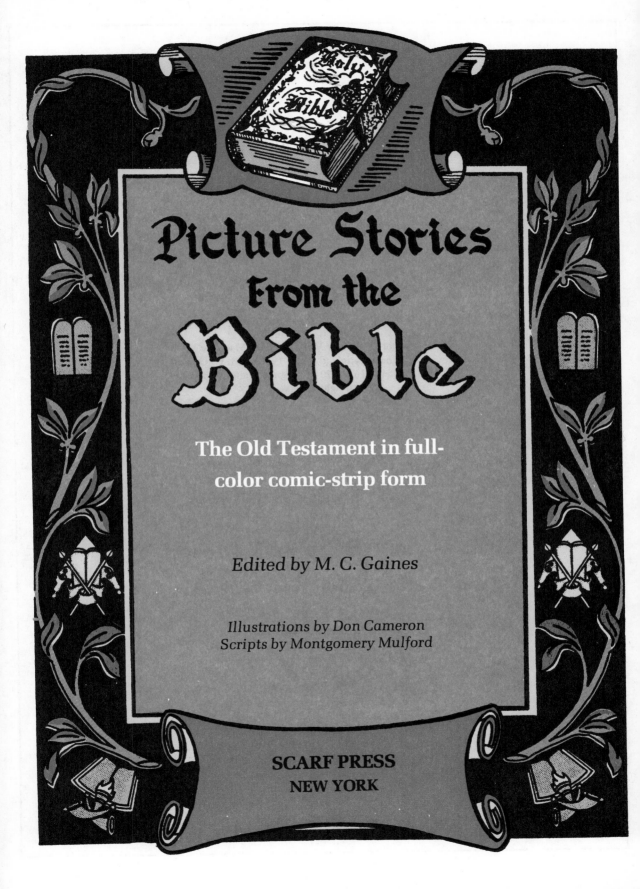

Picture Stories from the Bible

The Old Testament in full-color comic-strip form

Edited by M. C. Gaines

Illustrations by Don Cameron
Scripts by Montgomery Mulford

SCARF PRESS

NEW YORK

"To all our parents"

Scarf Press edition
Copyright © 1979 by Virginia Elaine Mac Adie
Previous edition copyright © 1942, 1943 by M. C. Gaines
Copyright renewed © 1970 by Virginia Elaine Mac Adie
All rights reserved

No part of this book may be reproduced
or transmitted in any form or by
any means without the
written permission of the publisher.

Published in the United States
and Canada by

Scarf Press
58 East 83rd Street
New York, New York 10028

Library of Congress Catalog Card Number: 79-66064
ISBN 0-934386-01-3

*In preparing this book, the
Protestant (King James), Catholic and Jewish
Publication Society versions were consulted.*

Printed in the United States of America
Color separations by Post Graphics Inc.

79 80 81 82 83 84   10 9 8 7 6 5 4 3 2 1

Contents

NOAH

ABRAHAM

JACOB

JOSEPH

MOSES

JOSHUA

DEBORAH

GIDEON

SAMSON

RUTH

SAMUEL

SAUL

DAVID

SOLOMON

ELIJAH

ELISHA

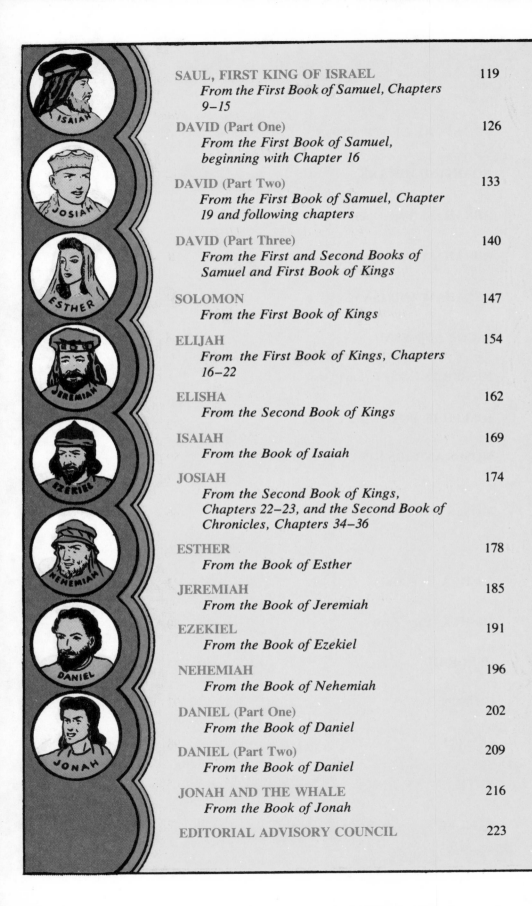

The Story of CREATION

FROM THE BOOK OF GENESIS CHAPTER 1 THROUGH 4

In The Beginning GOD Created The Heaven And The Earth

And The Earth Was Without Form, And Void; And Darkness Was Upon The Face Of The Deep ...

And God Said:— LET THERE BE LIGHT!—AND THE LIGHT SHALL BE CALLED DAY AND DARKNESS NIGHT!

AND GOD SAW THE LIGHT, THAT IT WAS GOOD ...

GOD MADE THE HEAVENS AND THE EARTH ON THE SECOND AND THIRD DAYS, AND THEN ...

THERE SHALL BE VEGETATION—GRASS, AND HERBS AND FRUIT!

ON THE FOURTH, FIFTH AND SIXTH DAYS, GOD CREATED THE SUN, MOON AND STARS, AND MADE THE FISH, BIRDS AND BEASTS!

BE FRUITFUL AND MULTIPLY!

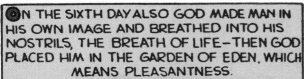

ON THE SIXTH DAY ALSO GOD MADE MAN IN HIS OWN IMAGE AND BREATHED INTO HIS NOSTRILS, THE BREATH OF LIFE—THEN GOD PLACED HIM IN THE GARDEN OF EDEN, WHICH MEANS PLEASANTNESS.

THIS IS A BEAUTIFUL WORLD!

LET MAN HAVE DOMINION OVER ALL THE EARTH!

GOD ASKED ONLY ONE THING OF ADAM FOR ALL HIS BLESSINGS—AND THAT WAS STRICT OBEDIENCE TO HIS WILL....

YOU MAY EAT THE FRUIT OF ANY TREE OF THE GARDEN BUT OF THE TREE OF THE KNOWLEDGE OF GOOD AND OF EVIL THOU SHALT NOT EAT!

THE FIRST MAN IN THE WORLD, CALLED ADAM, HAD TO GIVE NAMES TO ALL THE LIVING CREATURES ---

AND ON THE SEVENTH DAY GOD ENDED HIS WORK AND RESTED—AND GOD BLESSED THE SEVENTH DAY—AND MADE IT HOLY—BECAUSE ON THAT DAY HE RESTED FROM ALL HIS WORK

BUT ADAM WAS LONESOME; SO GOD CAUSED HIM TO SLEEP, AND TOOK ONE OF ADAM'S RIBS AND MADE A WOMAN

AWAKE, ADAM! YOU WILL NOT BE LONELY NOW FOR WE ARE TO BE MAN AND WIFE!

YOU ARE BONE OF MY BONE AND FLESH OF MY FLESH —I WILL CALL YOU EVE AND YOU SHALL BE MOTHER OF ALL LIVING---

AND AS ADAM SHOWED EVE ABOUT THE GARDEN OF EDEN, THEY CAME UPON THE TREE OF KNOWLEDGE~

THIS IS THE FORBIDDEN FRUIT!

BUT IT LOOKS SO GOOD, ADAM!

THE SERPENT, WHO HATED THE LORD GOD, TRIED TO MAKE EVE DISOBEY BY TELLING HER LIES ABOUT THE FRUIT--

SERPENT, WHAT DO YOU WANT OF ME?

THAT FRUIT IS FORBIDDEN--BUT I TELL YOU IT IS GOOD!

IF YOU EAT IT, YOU WILL BECOME VERY WISE AND KNOW ALL ABOUT EVERYTHING IN THE WORLD-TAKE A BITE!

NO -- THE LORD GOD SAID I MUST NOT!

JUST ONE BITE! THAT CAN'T DO ANY HARM!

HA! HA! SHE'S TEMPTED!

ADAM! ADAM! WAIT-- TASTE THIS FRUIT! IT'S GOOD!

GOD WON'T KNOW IF WE TAKE JUST ONE BITE!

HMM IT IS GOOD!

BECAUSE ADAM AND EVE DISOBEYED GOD, THEIR CONSCIENCES TROUBLED THEM-- .... THEY WANTED CLOTHES NOW, AND THEY MADE GARMENTS OUT OF FIG LEAVES--

LATER

IT'S GOD! HIDE, ADAM!

ADAM! ADAM!

HAVE YOU EATEN OF THE FRUIT I COMMANDED YOU NOT TO EAT?

EVE GAVE ME SOME, AND I DID EAT!

WHAT IS THIS YOU HAVE DONE?

O LORD, THE SERPENT TEMPTED ME AND I ATE!

YOU DISOBEYED ME! NOW YOU SHALL BOTH KNOW SUFFERING! FROM NOW ON YOU SHALL EARN YOUR LIVING BY HARD WORK! IN THE SWEAT OF YOUR FACE SHALL YOU EAT BREAD!

BEHOLD, YOU ARE BECOME ONE OF US, TO KNOW THE DIFFERENCE BETWEEN GOOD AND EVIL—AND NOW—YOU ARE BANISHED FROM THE GARDEN OF EDEN! GO!

LATER WHEN THEY HAD LEFT EDEN, TWO SONS WERE BORN TO ADAM AND EVE ~ THEIR NAMES WERE CAIN AND ABEL ~

WHEN I GROW UP I'LL WORK IN A FIELD. I LIKE TO WATCH THINGS GROW..

I'LL HAVE A FLOCK OF SHEEP! I LIKE ANIMALS.

AND SO THEY DID ---

CAIN IS A GOOD SON!

AND ABEL THE SHEPHERD IS A FINE LAD, TOO!

GOOD DAY, FATHER!

ONE DAY ABEL DECIDED TO MAKE AN OFFERING TO THE LORD - CAIN PLEDGED AN OFFERING TOO, BUT HIS HEART WAS NOT IN IT

FOR GOD'S GOODNESS I FEEL I SHOULD SACRIFICE A LAMB FROM MY FLOCK TO HIM!

O WELL, I CAN OFFER HIM SOME OF MY FRUIT!

I'LL NOT BE OUTDONE BY MY BROTHER, ABEL!

GOD, LOOKING INTO THEIR HEARTS, COMMENDS ABEL BUT NOT CAIN ---

ABEL, YOUR OFFERING IS PLEASING TO ME!

AND WHAT ABOUT MINE, LORD?

CAIN SLINKS AWAY ---

MY BROTHER IS THE FAVORED ONE OF GOD! MY OFFERING IS JUST AS GOOD!

WHY ARE YOU ANGRY, CAIN? IF YOU DO WELL, SHALL YOU NOT BE ACCEPTED?

JUST WAIT!

AFTER LONG WANDERINGS, CAIN WENT TO THE LAND OF NOD EAST OF EDEN. HERE HE FOUND AND TOOK UNTO HIMSELF A WIFE ~

I WANT YOU TO BE MY WIFE!

YES, CAIN, PERHAPS YOU MAY FIND PEACE!

A SON IS BORN TO THEM

AND YOUR FATHER HAS NAMED YOU ENOCH!

LATER ON, CAIN BUILT A CITY ~

I'M GOING TO BUILD A MIGHTY CITY, ENOCH, AND NAME IT AFTER YOU!

WILL HE REALLY DO IT?

MEANWHILE, GOD, TAKING PITY ON ADAM AND EVE, SENT THEM A THIRD SON, SETH ~

ADAM! WE ARE TO HAVE ANOTHER SON!

A CHILD TO COMFORT OUR LONELINESS - WE'LL NAME HIM SETH!

LATER, MANY MORE SONS AND DAUGHTERS WERE BORN TO THEM AND TO SETH ~

ADAM AND HIS

DESCENDANTS LIVED TO GRAND OLD AGES · · · · · · ·

AND AS MEN BEGAN TO MULTIPLY ON THE FACE OF THE EARTH, THEY TOOK WIVES, AND SOME OF THE CHILDREN BORN TO THEM BECAME MIGHTY BIBLE HEROES, LIKE NOAH, ABRAHAM AND MOSES · · · · ·

for

"THERE WERE GIANTS ON THE EARTH IN THOSE DAYS" · · · · ·

NOAH AND HIS ARK

ARRANGED FROM THE STORY OF NOAH IN THE BOOK OF GENESIS, CHAPTERS 6 THROUGH 9.

GOD SAW THAT WICKEDNESS WAS GREAT ON EARTH, AND GRIEVED---

I WILL DESTROY MAN AND BEAST AND ALL CREEPING THINGS - FOWLS OF THE AIR - FOR I AM SORRY THAT I HAVE MADE THEM!

BUT ONE MAN ALONE WAS UPRIGHT, AND LOVED HIS GOD - HE WAS NOAH ~~~

MY SONS, SHEM, HAM AND JAPHETH, LOVE THY GOD ALWAYS, AND DO WHAT IS GOOD AND RIGHT!

GOD, IN HIS DISPLEASURE, SAID TO NOAH ~~

THE END OF ALL FLESH IS COME! FOR THE EARTH IS FILLED WITH VIOLENCE THROUGH THEM. BEHOLD - I WILL DESTROY EVERYTHING!

YOU I SHALL SPARE! MAKE AN ARK OF GOPHER-WOOD, THREE STORIES HIGH - MAKE ROOMS IN IT - CUT A DOOR AND MAKE ONLY ONE WINDOW!

MUST I GO ALONE?

WHEN I SEND THE FLOOD, YOU AND YOUR SONS AND ALL YOUR RELATIVES SHALL GO WITH YOU INTO THE ARK, AND YOU SHALL TAKE FOOD FOR ALL!

SOME OF EVERY KIND OF LIVING THING SHALL GO WITH YOU INTO THE ARK — A MALE AND A FEMALE — AND YOU SHALL HAVE FOOD ENOUGH FOR ALL!

NOAH AND HIS SONS, WENT TO WORK AT ONCE, TO BUILD THE ARK~~~

NOW, THAT THE ARK IS FINISHED, WE MUST ROUND UP SOME OF EVERY CREATURE ON THE EARTH, AND LEAD THEM INTO THE ARK!

AFTER SEVEN DAYS, ALL WAS READY ~~~

I HAVE OBEYED THE LORD, AND ALL MY FAMILY, AND SOME OF EVERY CREATURE ARE WITHIN!

MEANWHILE, IN THE NEARBY TOWN ~~~

HEAR THE LATEST, MEN?- CRAZY OLD NOAH'S GOT HIS RELATIVES SHUT IN HIS ARK WITH HIM! WHAT'S WRONG WITH HIM?

HEE! SAME THING THAT'S WRONG WITH ME-OLD AGE!

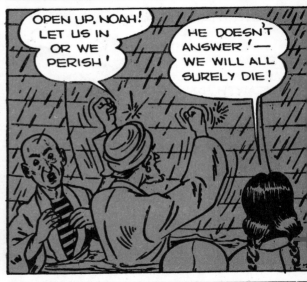

BUT THE RAVEN IS BEWILDERED! HE FINDS NO LAND, AND FLIES IN CIRCLES ----

NOW, I SHALL SEND FORTH THE DOVE TO SEEK LAND WHICH WAS NOT SEEN YESTERDAY!

LATER, THE DOVE COMES BACK ~~~

WE MUST WAIT AGAIN — WE SHALL WAIT ANOTHER SEVEN DAYS!

SO THE DOVE WAS RELEASED ONCE AGAIN AND FLEW OFF AND WAS GONE. BUT THIS TIME IT FOUND LAND ~

LOOK! - THE DOVE HAS BROUGHT A LEAF! - IT IS A SIGN OF LAND!

YES!

SO WE KNOW THAT THE WATERS ARE GOING DOWN, AND THAT LAND ONCE AGAIN IS APPEARING!

THEN WE MAY SOON LEAVE THE ARK AND MAKE NEW HOMES FOR US ALL!

SOON THE WATERS WENT DOWN, LEAVING THE ARK ON TOP OF MOUNT ARARAT ~~

THEN GOD SPOKE TO NOAH ONCE AGAIN, AS THE EARTH DRIED UP ~~

GO OUT OF THE ARK, YOU AND ALL THE REST, AND LIVE AGAIN UPON THE EARTH AND MULTIPLY!

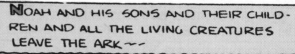

NEVER AGAIN WILL THE WORLD BE FLOODED— IN THIS WAY SHALL I NEVER AGAIN DESTROY THE EARTH —IT IS MY PLEDGE TO YOU, NOAH, AND YOUR DESCENDANTS!

NOAH AND HIS SONS AND THEIR CHILDREN AND ALL THE LIVING CREATURES LEAVE THE ARK ~~

THE LORD SPEAKS AGAIN ~~~

IT SHALL BE A TOKEN TO YOU THAT MANKIND WILL NOT BE DESTROYED, BUT WILL LIVE IN HOPE OF A BETTER WORLD!

SO THE RAINBOW OF HOPE WAS BORN AND POINTED THE WAY TO NOAH ~~~

So the world was cleansed, and the sons of Noah built new homes, and all the creatures multiplied and inhabited the earth---

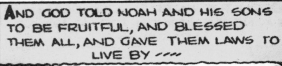

And God told Noah and his sons to be fruitful, and blessed them all, and gave them laws to live by ---

REPLENISH THE EARTH, BUT KILL YOU NOT ONE ANOTHER! - FOR WHO SHEDS BLOOD, HIS BLOOD SHALL BE SHED ALSO!

Noah fulfills God's commands... in his old age he plants a vineyard!

FATHER, ARE YOU HAPPY NOW?

YES, LET US GO HOME, MY SONS!

Noah lived to be nine hundred and fifty years old and then he died ·····

WE MUST GO ON LIVING GOOD LIVES, THO OUR FATHER IS GONE FOR GOD CHOSE HIM OF ALL MANKIND TO PRESERVE THE HUMAN RACE. WE MUST HONOR HIS NAME BY LIVING RIGHTLY!

END

The Story of ABRAHAM

THE FOUNDER OF THE HEBREW NATION

ABRAHAM WAS CALLED ABRAM ("ESTEEMED OR HIGH FATHER") IN THE EARLY YEARS OF HIS LIFE — HIS NAME WAS CHANGED TO ABRAHAM, MEANING "FATHER OF A MULTITUDE" WHEN GOD PROMISED HIM AND HIS DESCENDANTS THE LAND OF CANAAN ~~~

FROM THE BOOK OF GENESIS CHAP. XI THRU CHAP. XV.

TERAH, THE FATHER OF ABRAM, LIVED HAPPILY IN CHALDEA, WITH HIS THREE SONS, ABRAM'S WIFE, SARAI, AND THEIR NEPHEW, LOT ~~~

BUT WHEN HARAN, ONE OF ABRAM'S BROTHERS DIED, THE FAMILY GREW RESTLESS ~~~

YES, SINCE MY SON HARAN DIED, I AM NO LONGER HAPPY HERE!

WE COULD FIND A BETTER PLACE TO LIVE!

LET US GO TO OTHER LANDS!

SO THEY ALL LEFT THE CITY OF UR, WHERE ABRAM'S FATHER HAD BEEN WORSHIPPING FALSE GODS ~~~

YES, SARAI I HOPE I NEVER SEE THOSE IDOLS AGAIN -- WE WORSHIP THE TRUE GOD!

NOW THAT WE'VE LEFT THAT IDOL-WORSHIPPING PLACE MAYBE TERAH WILL TURN FROM FALSE GODS TO THE TRUE GOD!

THEY FINALLY CAME TO THE LAND OF HARAN—HERE THEY PITCHED THEIR TENTS AND LIVED FOR FIFTEEN YEARS IN PEACE AND HAPPINESS ...

I HAVE BEEN HAPPY HERE IN THIS NEW LAND BUT I KNOW I SHALL NOT BE WITH YOU MUCH LONGER!

DON'T SAY THAT, FATHER!

TERAH DIED AT A GRAND OLD AGE -- ABRAM AND LOT MOURNED HIM ...

A LONG AND USEFUL LIFE! — I'M GLAD HE LEFT HIS FALSE GODS AND TURNED TO THE TRUE ONE!

WITH GRANDFATHER GONE OUR HOME WILL BE BROKEN UP— WHERE SHALL I GO?

PLEASE STAY WITH US — YOU ARE MY BROTHER'S SON, LOT, AND AS DEAR TO ME AS MY OWN. INDEED— GOD HAS GIVEN US NO OTHER CHILDREN!

DO STAY, LOT!

I'LL STAY!

AND GOD SPOKE TO ABRAM IN HIS GRIEF ...

LEAVE YOUR FATHER'S HOUSE AND GO INTO A LAND I WILL SHOW YOU -- THERE YOU SHALL FOUND A GREAT NATION -- THROUGH YOU ALL THE FAMILIES OF THE EARTH SHALL BE BLESSED!

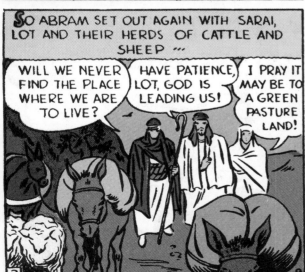

SO ABRAM SET OUT AGAIN WITH SARAI, LOT AND THEIR HERDS OF CATTLE AND SHEEP ...

WILL WE NEVER FIND THE PLACE WHERE WE ARE TO LIVE?

HAVE PATIENCE, LOT, GOD IS LEADING US!

I PRAY IT MAY BE TO A GREEN PASTURE LAND!

AT LAST THEY CAME TO THE FAIR LAND OF CANAAN ...

IT IS JUST AS BEAUTIFUL AS I DREAMED IT WOULD BE!

IT LOOKS SO FRESH AND PEACEFUL!

AND GOD APPEARED AGAIN UNTO ABRAM---

UNTO YOUR DESCENDANTS WILL I GIVE THIS LAND!

IN GRATITUDE, ABRAM BUILT AN ALTAR TO THE LORD ---

I THANK YOU, GOD, FOR BRINGING US SO FAR ALONG THE WAY!

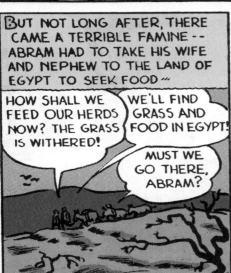

BUT NOT LONG AFTER, THERE CAME A TERRIBLE FAMINE -- ABRAM HAD TO TAKE HIS WIFE AND NEPHEW TO THE LAND OF EGYPT TO SEEK FOOD ---

HOW SHALL WE FEED OUR HERDS NOW? THE GRASS IS WITHERED!

WE'LL FIND GRASS AND FOOD IN EGYPT!

MUST WE GO THERE, ABRAM?

THOUGH SARAI DID NOT WANT TO GO TO EGYPT, THEY SET OUT ---

I FEAR THE WAY THESE MEN LOOK AT ME!-THEY ARE PHARAOH'S GUARDS!

THEY MAY WANT TO KILL ME IF THEY THINK YOU ARE MY WIFE--TELL THEM YOU ARE MY SISTER

SARAI WAS THE DAUGHTER OF ABRAM'S BROTHER, AND THE HEBREW WORD "NIECE" COULD ALSO MEAN "SISTER".

PHARAOH'S MEN DID SEIZE THE LOVELY SARAI ---

COME, WITH US!

BUT-

WE'LL TAKE YOU TO THE PHARAOH!

SHE IS THE SISTER OF ABRAM, FROM THE LAND OF CANAAN!

SO YOU CAME TO EGYPT FOR FOOD. WELL, YOU SHALL HAVE PLENTY-AND OXEN, CAMELS AND SERVANTS BESIDES!

OUTSIDE, ABRAM, GRIEF STRICKEN, PRAYS TO THE LORD—

PLEASE SAVE SARAI! IF THE PHARAOH DISCOVERS NOW THAT SHE IS MY WIFE, HE MAY KILL US BOTH!

PHARAOH AND ALL HIS COURT WERE SUDDENLY STRICKEN WITH A GREAT PLAGUE—

O SARAI, I'M SO ILL—CALL MY PHYSICIAN! —PERHAPS I'VE BEEN POISONED!

YES, SIRE!

NOT POISONED, PUNISHED!

NEARLY THE WHOLE COURT IS ILL!

I CANNOT UNDERSTAND IT! —WHY DOES THE PLAGUE STRIKE THE PHARAOH'S COURT AND NO OTHER PLACE?

I WILL TELL YOU—I AM ABRAM'S WIFE —NOT HIS SISTER!

WHY WAS I NOT TOLD OF THIS! GUARDS, BRING ABRAM TO ME!

SHORTLY AFTER—

ABRAM, YOU MUST ASK GOD TO LIFT THIS PLAGUE! —TAKE YOUR WIFE, AND RETURN TO CANAAN KEEP THE SHEEP AND ALL THE GIFTS I GAVE—BUT LEAVE!

WE SHALL GO THIS DAY, PHARAOH!

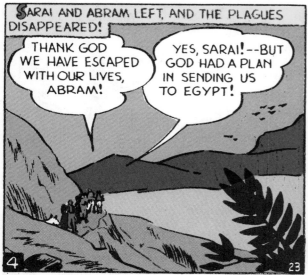

SARAI AND ABRAM LEFT, AND THE PLAGUES DISAPPEARED!

THANK GOD WE HAVE ESCAPED WITH OUR LIVES, ABRAM!

YES, SARAI!—BUT GOD HAD A PLAN IN SENDING US TO EGYPT!

AND SO ABRAM AND HIS FAMILY RETURNED TO THE LAND OF CANAAN WITH THE PHARAOH'S GIFTS—

BACK IN CANAAN, AS THEIR FLOCKS INCREASED, LOT'S AND ABRAM'S HERDSMEN FOUGHT ABOUT THE GOOD GRAZING LAND

GET YOUR SHEEP OFF THIS LAND — WE WERE HERE FIRST!

GET YOURS OFF OR I'LL HIT YOU AGAIN!

ABRAM AND LOT BREAK UP THE FIGHTING —

STOP THIS FIGHTING!

LET THERE BE NO STRIFE BETWEEN US OR OUR MEN, FOR WE ARE KINSMEN!

SEE, LOT, THERE IS PLENTY OF LAND FOR US BOTH — YOU TAKE YOUR CHOICE!

THANK YOU, UNCLE, I CHOOSE THIS FERTILE PLAIN OF JORDAN TO THE EAST!

GOOD! — THAT LAND **IS** FERTILE — BUT BEWARE THE WICKED MEN OF SODOM!

AND GOD RENEWS HIS PROMISE —

ALL THE LAND YOU SEE, I WILL GIVE TO YOU AND YOUR CHILDREN FOREVER — I WILL MAKE YOUR CHILDREN AS THE DUST OF THE EARTH, SO THAT IF A MAN CAN NUMBER THE DUST OF EARTH, THEN SHALL YOUR CHILDREN BE NUMBERED!

BUT LOT WITH HIS WIFE IN HIS NEW HOME SOON RAN INTO TROUBLE -- WARRING KINGS LAID WASTE THE LANDS OF SODOM AND SALEM ~~

TAKE ALL THEIR SHEEP!

BUT WHY ATTACK ME? I HAVEN'T HARMED YOU!

WHO IS TO STOP US?

LOT IS TAKEN PRISONER ~

HERE'S A GOOD STRONG ONE - I'LL TAKE HIM FOR MY SLAVE!

OH, LOT, WHERE ARE THEY TAKING YOU?

GET WORD TO ABRAM - HE'LL SAVE US!

ONE OF LOT'S SERVANTS MANAGES TO ESCAPE ~

IT'S GOOD THEY DON'T WATCH ME AS CLOSELY AS LOT - NOW TO FREE MY FEET AND FETCH HELP!

THE SERVANT MAKES HIS WAY TO ABRAM

LOT AND HIS FAMILY ARE CAPTURED - I ESCAPED AND CAME HERE TO LET YOU KNOW!

I WILL MAKE AN ARMY OUT OF MY FAITHFUL SERVANTS, AND WE'LL RESCUE LOT!

ABRAM, WITH HIS ARMED SERVANTS, RIDES TO RESCUE THE PRISONERS ~~

TAKE HALF THE MEN AND ATTACK FROM THE RIGHT, WHILE I STRIKE ON THE LEFT!

FINE! WE'LL THROW THEM INTO A PANIC!

THE NIGHT ATTACK CARRIES ALL BEFORE IT ~

RUN! FLEE! WE ARE OVERPOWERED!

SO ABRAM RECAPTURED THE STOLEN GOODS AND SET THE PRISONERS FREE ~~

I KNEW YOU WOULD COME AND SAVE ME, ABRAM!

WHY SHOULDN'T I? YOU ARE LIKE A SON TO ME LOT!

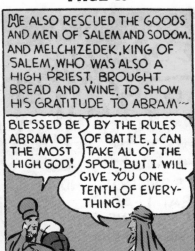

HE ALSO RESCUED THE GOODS AND MEN OF SALEM AND SODOM. AND MELCHIZEDEK, KING OF SALEM, WHO WAS ALSO A HIGH PRIEST, BROUGHT BREAD AND WINE, TO SHOW HIS GRATITUDE TO ABRAM ~~

BLESSED BE ABRAM OF THE MOST HIGH GOD!

BY THE RULES OF BATTLE, I CAN TAKE ALL OF THE SPOIL, BUT I WILL GIVE YOU ONE TENTH OF EVERYTHING!

BUT ABRAM WOULD HAVE NOTHING TO DO WITH THE WICKED KING OF SODOM ~~

YOU HAVE RESCUED MY PEOPLE AND GOODS ABRAM- KEEP THE GOODS AS A REWARD!

NO, LEST YOU THINK THAT YOU, NOT GOD, MADE ME RICH!

AND GOD WAS GREATLY PLEASED WITH ABRAM AND WHEN ABRAM DESIRED A SON AND HEIR, THIS WAS GOD'S PROMISE ~~

LOOK NOW TOWARD HEAVEN AND COUNT, IF YOU CAN, THE STARS— SO IN NUMBER SHALL YOUR CHILDREN AND YOUR CHILDREN'S CHILDREN BE!

A DEEP SLEEP FELL ON ABRAM, AS GOD'S VOICE CONTINUED --

YOUR CHILDREN SHALL BE STRANGERS AND OPPRESSED IN A LAND THAT IS NOT THEIRS BUT THEY SHALL GO FORTH AGAIN, - FOR I SHALL GIVE THEM THIS LAND -- THIS IS MY COVENANT!

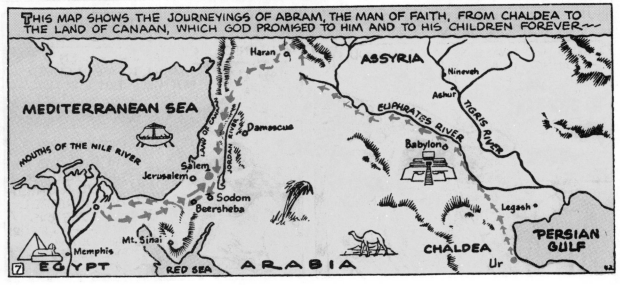

THIS MAP SHOWS THE JOURNEYINGS OF ABRAM, THE MAN OF FAITH, FROM CHALDEA TO THE LAND OF CANAAN, WHICH GOD PROMISED TO HIM AND TO HIS CHILDREN FOREVER ~~

Haran

ASSYRIA

Nineveh

Ashur

MEDITERRANEAN SEA

EUPHRATES RIVER

TIGRIS RIVER

Damascus

LAND OF CANAAN

JORDAN RIVER

Babylon

MOUTHS OF THE NILE RIVER

Salem

Jerusalem

Sodom

Beersheba

Legash

PERSIAN GULF

Memphis

Mt. Sinai

CHALDEA

Ur

EGYPT

RED SEA

ARABIA

The Story of ABRAHAM

Part Two

ABRAHAM, THROUGH HIS WISDOM AND COURAGE, BECAME A GREAT LEADER OF HIS PEOPLE, BUT IN ONE THING ONLY WAS HE DISAPPOINTED — HE HAD NO SON

FROM THE BOOK OF GENESIS, CHAP. 16 THRU 21

SARAI, FEARING THAT SHE COULD NOT HAVE A SON, URGED ABRAM TO TAKE A SECOND WIFE, ACCORDING TO THE LAW OF THE COUNTRY ~

TAKE ANOTHER WIFE, ABRAM — HAGAR, MY EGYPTIAN MAID — PERHAPS WE MAY OBTAIN CHILDREN BY HER!

IF YOU WISH IT, SARAI!

AND SARAI AND I WILL TREAT YOUR CHILDREN AS OUR OWN, HAGAR — THEY SHALL BEAR OUR NAME, AND INHERIT ALL MY POSSESSIONS!

SO BE IT!

BUT AFTERWARD HAGAR BEGAN TO DESPISE HER MISTRESS SARAI ~~~

SEND HER AWAY — I CANNOT BEAR TO HAVE HER HERE ANYMORE!

DO AS YOU THINK BEST!

WHEN SARAI PUNISHED HAGAR FOR HER INSOLENCE HAGAR FLED INTO THE WILDERNESS ~~

SARAI HAS BEEN CRUEL TO ME — I COULD NOT HELP BUT RUN AWAY ——

RETURN TO SARAI AND DO AS SHE TELLS YOU — YOU SHALL HAVE A CHILD — CALL HIM ISHMAEL — FOR THAT MEANS THE LORD HAS HEARD YOU IN YOUR TROUBLE!

HAGAR GIVES ABRAM A SON, ISHMAEL ~

AT LAST I HAVE A SON!

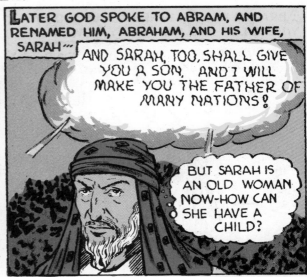

LATER GOD SPOKE TO ABRAM, AND RENAMED HIM, ABRAHAM, AND HIS WIFE, SARAH ~

AND SARAH, TOO, SHALL GIVE YOU A SON, AND I WILL MAKE YOU THE FATHER OF MANY NATIONS!

BUT SARAH IS AN OLD WOMAN NOW-HOW CAN SHE HAVE A CHILD?

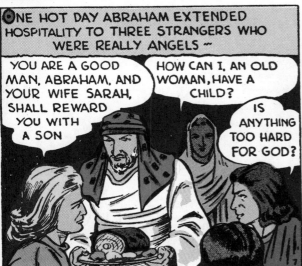

ONE HOT DAY ABRAHAM EXTENDED HOSPITALITY TO THREE STRANGERS WHO WERE REALLY ANGELS ~

YOU ARE A GOOD MAN, ABRAHAM, AND YOUR WIFE SARAH, SHALL REWARD YOU WITH A SON

HOW CAN I, AN OLD WOMAN, HAVE A CHILD?

IS ANYTHING TOO HARD FOR GOD?

LATER..

OUR THANKS FOR YOUR HOSPITALITY!

WHICH IS THE ROAD TO SODOM?

I WILL SHOW YOU THE WAY!

THE ANGELS GO ON THEIR WAY TOWARD THE WICKED CITY, BUT THE VOICE OF GOD HALTS ABRAHAM ON THE ROAD ~

LISTEN, ABRAHAM, I PLAN TO DESTROY THAT WICKED CITY OF SODOM!

ABRAHAM IS CONCERNED ABOUT SODOM WHERE LOT AND HIS FAMILY NOW LIVE ~~~

BUT WILL YOU DESTROY THE GOOD PEOPLE WITH THE WICKED?

IF I FIND FIFTY GOOD MEN IN SODOM I SHALL SPARE THE WHOLE CITY FOR THEIR SAKES!

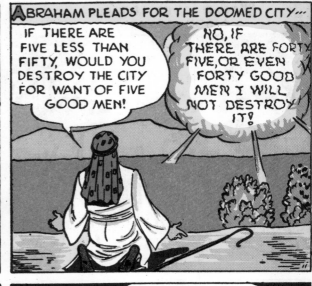

ABRAHAM PLEADS FOR THE DOOMED CITY ~~~

IF THERE ARE FIVE LESS THAN FIFTY, WOULD YOU DESTROY THE CITY FOR WANT OF FIVE GOOD MEN!

NO, IF THERE ARE FORTY FIVE, OR EVEN FORTY GOOD MEN I WILL NOT DESTROY IT!

ABRAHAM CONTINUES TO PLEAD WITH GOD~

DO NOT BE ANGRY WITH ME! ~ PERHAPS YOU WILL FIND THIRTY GOOD MEN THERE!

FOR THIRTY ~ EVEN FOR TWENTY GOOD MEN I WILL SPARE SODOM!

BUT LORD, SUPPOSE THERE ARE ONLY TEN GOOD MEN IN SODOM!

GOD GRANTS ABRAM'S LAST PLEA ~~

EVEN FOR TEN I WILL SPARE THE CITY!

THANK YOU, LORD!

SOON AFTERWARD, IN SODOM, LOT SEES TWO FOOTSORE TRAVELERS AT THE GATE OF THE CITY ~~~

YOU LOOK TIRED, STRANGERS~ ~COME TO MY HOUSE ~ WE WILL GIVE YOU FOOD AND DRINK AND SHELTER FOR THE NIGHT!

YOU ARE VERY KIND!

PAGE 29

SOMETIME LATER ---

IT'S WONDERFUL -- I HAVE A BABY, ISAAC -- AS GOD PROMISED!

I AM SO PROUD!

BUT SARAH HAS NO PEACE WITH HAGAR AND HER SON, ISHMAEL, IN THE HOUSE ---

SILLY TO MAKE SUCH A FUSS OVER A BABY!

NOW HAGAR'S SON MOCKS AT ME!" I WON'T BEAR THIS ANY LONGER!

ABRAHAM, YOU MUST SEND HAGAR AWAY!

IF YOU WISH IT, SARAH!

I AM SORRY TO SEND YOU AWAY, BUT IT MUST BE! TAKE THIS BREAD AND WATER WITH YOU, AND GOD PROTECT YOU!

I'LL GO INTO THE WILDERNESS!

THEIR WATER GONE, HAGAR AND ISHMAEL WANDER THROUGH THE WILDERNESS, THIRSTY AND EXHAUSTED ---

WATER! MOTHER! GIVE ME WATER!

I CAN'T BEAR TO SEE HIM SUFFER!

AN ANGEL OF GOD APPEARS AND SHOWS THEM WATER BEHIND A SHRUB ---

WATER! NOW ISHMAEL WILL NOT DIE!

DON'T BE AFRAID, HAGAR -- GOD HEARD ISHMAEL'S CRIES, AND WILL MAKE HIM A GREAT MAN!

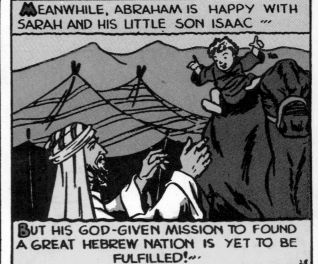

MEANWHILE, ABRAHAM IS HAPPY WITH SARAH AND HIS LITTLE SON ISAAC ---

BUT HIS GOD-GIVEN MISSION TO FOUND A GREAT HEBREW NATION IS YET TO BE FULFILLED! ---

THE STORY OF ABRAHAM

AND ISAAC

FROM THE BOOK OF GENESIS, CHAP. XXI THROUGH XXV

PART THREE

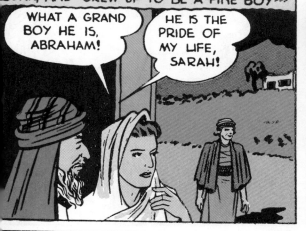

ABRAHAM AND SARAH FOR MANY YEARS HAD DESIRED A SON — AT LAST ISAAC WAS BORN, AND GREW UP TO BE A FINE BOY...

WHAT A GRAND BOY HE IS, ABRAHAM!

HE IS THE PRIDE OF MY LIFE, SARAH!

GOD DETERMINED TO TEST ABRAHAM'S FAITH — ONE DAY AS HE WAS WALKING IN A GROVE OF TREES HE HAD PLANTED...

ABRAHAM!

HERE I AM!

TAKE ISAAC, YOUR ONLY SON WHOM YOU LOVE, AND GO TO A MOUNTAIN I WILL TELL YOU OF — AND THERE SACRIFICE HIM TO ME!

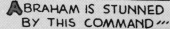

ABRAHAM IS STUNNED BY THIS COMMAND...

NOTHING WAS LACKING TO ME BUT A SON, AND EVEN THAT GOD GRANTED ME — NOW HE WANTS HIM BACK — IT IS HARD!

—BUT ABRAHAM GATHERS HIS STRENGTH TO OBEY...

BUT LET ME ALWAYS REMEMBER, LORD, THE JOY MY CHILD HAS BROUGHT ME!--AND LET ME ALWAYS REMEMBER THE THANKS I OWE TO YOU! AND NOW GIVE ME STRENGTH TO OBEY YOUR WISH!

WHERE ARE WE GOING FATHER?

THE LORD HAS COMMANDED ME TO MAKE A SACRIFICE TO HIM—COME!

BUT WHERE IS THE LAMB FOR THE SACRIFICE, FATHER?

THE LORD WILL PROVIDE, MY SON!

WAIT HERE FOR ME—MY SON AND I ARE GOING UP ON THE MOUNTAIN TO WORSHIP!

BUT, FATHER, HOW CAN YOU MAKE A SACRIFICE IF YOU DON'T HAVE A LAMB?

MY SON, YOU ARE THE LAMB!

ISAAC WAS TERRIFIED AT FIRST, BUT...

GOD KNEW WHAT I HELD MOST DEAR, AND THIS HE CAME IN A VISION TO ASK ME FOR! —FORGIVE ME, SON!

IF GOD BIDS YOU THEN DO IT, FATHER-I SHALL NOT BE AFRAID, FOR GOD WISHES YOUR GOOD AND MINE!

WAIT, ABRAHAM!

IT IS THE VOICE OF GOD'S ANGEL!

I WANTED TO TEST YOU, ABRAHAM. I DO NOT WANT YOU TO SACRIFICE YOUR SON — I WANTED ONLY TO FIND OUT IF YOU WOULD TRUST ME!

ABRAHAM AND ISAAC KNEEL IN PRAYER ~

THANKS, O LORD, FOR YOUR MERCY AND FOR THIS LESSON! — FROM NOW ON LET NO MAN SACRIFICE ANOTHER IN YOUR NAME!

MAY OUR CHILDREN'S CHILDREN REMEMBER FOREVER! GOD ASKS US TO GIVE UP WHAT IS DEAR TO US NEVER WHAT IS DEAR TO ANOTHER!

THEN ABRAHAM SAW A RAM CAUGHT IN THE THICKET BY ITS HORNS, AND SACRIFICED THE RAM ~

I WAS WILLING TO GIVE YOU TO GOD, BUT NOW I CAN KEEP YOU!

I KNEW I WOULD NOT BE AFRAID, FATHER!

SARAH PASSED AWAY AND ISAAC GREW TO MANHOOD. ABRAHAM CALLED HIS SERVANT, ELIEZER ~

I'M GETTING OLD AND I WANT MY SON TO MARRY — YOU MUST GO TO THE LAND WE COME FROM AND THERE FIND A WIFE FOR HIM — BUT SHE MUST COME FROM AMONG MY KINDRED!

I PROMISE!

ABRAHAM'S SERVANT SETS OFF ON HIS MISSION WITH A CARAVAN OF TEN CAMELS ~

I AM GOING TO THE CITY WHERE NAHOR, THE BROTHER OF ABRAHAM LIVES — MAY GOD REVEAL TO ME THE WOMAN I SEEK FOR ISAAC!

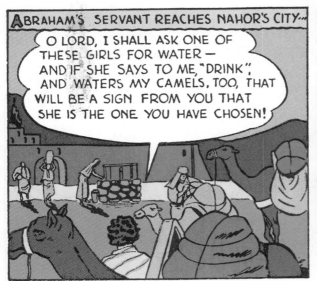

ABRAHAM'S SERVANT REACHES NAHOR'S CITY...

O LORD, I SHALL ASK ONE OF THESE GIRLS FOR WATER — AND IF SHE SAYS TO ME, "DRINK", AND WATERS MY CAMELS, TOO, THAT WILL BE A SIGN FROM YOU THAT SHE IS THE ONE YOU HAVE CHOSEN!

REBEKAH APPROACHES THE WELL WITH A WATER-PITCHER ON HER SHOULDER ...

WHAT A BEAUTIFUL GIRL! —BUT— WOULD SHE BE KIND, TOO? NOW TO TEST HER!

PLEASE GIVE ME A DRINK OF YOUR WATER — I'M THIRSTY!

GLADLY, SIR- YOU LOOK ALL HOT AND DUSTY FROM TRAVEL! -YOU MUST BE VERY TIRED!

REBEKAH MEETS THE TEST ...

LET ME ALSO WATER YOUR CAMELS -- HOW THIRSTY THEY MUST BE!

IT IS A SIGN, O LORD! SHE IS AS GOOD AS SHE IS BEAUTIFUL!

THE SERVANT IS NOW SURE HE HAS FOUND THE RIGHT WIFE FOR ISAAC ...

THESE ARE GIFTS, IN GRATITUDE- TELL ME, WHOSE DAUGHTER ARE YOU?

I AM REBEKAH, NAHOR'S GRAND-DAUGHTER. -MY FATHER IS BETHUEL, THE SYRIAN!

IS THERE ROOM IN YOUR FATHER'S HOUSE FOR US TO LODGE TONIGHT?

THERE IS MY BROTHER LABAN-- I'LL ASK HIM!

SHE IS BETHUEL'S DAUGHTER! - HOW WONDERFUL! - BLESSED BE THE LORD GOD WHO HAS LED ME TO THE HOUSE OF ABRAHAM'S KINSMAN!

COME STRAIGHT TO OUR HOUSE! YOU ARE WELCOME! A GOOD DINNER IS READY AND FEED FOR YOUR CAMELS!

I WILL NOT EAT TILL I HAVE TOLD MY ERRAND!

IN BETHUEL'S HOUSE

FIRST I MUST SPEAK. BETHUEL, YOUR UNCLE ABRAHAM HAS SENT ME TO FIND A WIFE FROM AMONG HIS KINSMEN, FOR HIS SON ISAAC— HE PROMISED THAT GOD WOULD GUIDE ME--

—AND WHEN I CAME TO THE WELL I ASKED GOD FOR A SIGN—WHEN REBEKAH GAVE WATER TO ME AND MY CAMELS I KNEW SHE WAS GOD'S CHOICE—WILL YOU LET HER WED HIM?

WILL YOU GO WITH THIS MAN AND MARRY ISAAC?

I WILL GO!

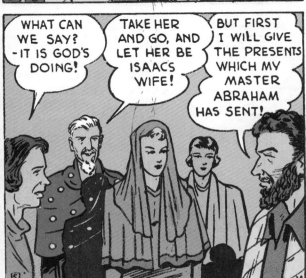

WHAT CAN WE SAY? -IT IS GOD'S DOING!

TAKE HER AND GO, AND LET HER BE ISAACS WIFE!

BUT FIRST I WILL GIVE THE PRESENTS WHICH MY MASTER ABRAHAM HAS SENT!

SO ABRAHAM'S SERVANT STARTED HOMEWARD WITH REBEKAH AND HER MAIDS AND A LONG TRAIN OF CAMELS ʼʼʼ

AND AS WE RIDE, WILL YOU TELL ME ABOUT ISAAC?

NOW REBEKAH UNVEILS HERSELF ~

OH, BUT YOU ARE BEAUTIFUL, REBEKAH!

AND YOU ARE KIND, MY BELOVED..I KNOW WE SHALL BE HAPPY TOGETHER!

NOW THAT ISAAC WAS MARRIED, ABRAHAM WAS LONELY WITHOUT HIS WIFE SARAH, SO HE MET AND MARRIED KETURAH, WHO BORE HIM A LARGE FAMILY. BUT OF ALL HIS SONS, HE STILL LOVED ISAAC BEST ~

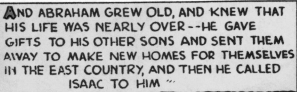

AND ABRAHAM GREW OLD, AND KNEW THAT HIS LIFE WAS NEARLY OVER -- HE GAVE GIFTS TO HIS OTHER SONS AND SENT THEM AWAY TO MAKE NEW HOMES FOR THEMSELVES IN THE EAST COUNTRY, AND THEN HE CALLED ISAAC TO HIM ~

MY SON, I LEAVE TO YOU EVERYTHING THAT I HAVE - IF ONLY I COULD SEE MY OTHER SON ISHMAEL, I WOULD BE HAPPY IN MY LAST DAYS!

LOOK, FATHER, WHO STANDS BESIDE THE TENT!

I AM ISHMAEL, THE HUNTER - I HAVE COME BACK FROM THE WILDERNESS TO VISIT MY FATHER!

MY SON YOU HAVE BEEN AWAY A LONG TIME!

NOW I HAVE SEEN YOU AGAIN ISHMAEL, I CAN DIE CONTENT!

AND I LIVE CONTENT, FATHER, HAVING SEEN YOU!

SO ABRAHAM, ANCESTOR OF THE HEBREWS, WAS GATHERED TO HIS FATHERS ~

I MUST GO BACK TO MY FORESTS AGAIN - BUT I AM GLAD I HAVE COME TO KNOW AND LOVE YOU, BROTHER ISAAC, AND MY FATHER ABRAHAM - I SHALL ALWAYS REMEMBER HIM!

END

The Story of JACOB and ESAU
THE TWINS
FROM GENESIS XXV-XXXIII

THERE WAS GREAT REJOICING IN THE HOME OF ISAAC AND HIS WIFE REBEKAH ON THE DAY THEIR SONS WERE BORN~AS GOD HAD PROMISED, THE BABIES WERE TWINS~

WHAT WILL YOU CALL THEM ISAAC?

THIS FELLOW IS SO RED AND HAIRY, WE'LL CALL HIM ESAU-THAT WORD MEANS HAIRY!

- AND THE OTHER BABY, WHO WAS BORN LATER, WE'LL CALL JACOB!

THE TWO BOYS GREW UP TO BE UNLIKE IN THEIR WAYS~

OFF TO THE HUNT! WONDER IF I'LL GET A DEER!

I JUST STAY HERE AND WORK!-YET ESAU IS THE ONE FATHER LIKES!

BUT ESAU COULD FIND NOTHING TO SHOOT AND CAME HOME DAYS LATER, ALMOST STARVING~

THIS LENTIL POTTAGE SMELLS GOOD-WONDER WHERE ESAU- WHY, HERE YOU ARE!

I'M NEARLY DEAD OF HUNGER- GIVE ME FOOD, QUICK!

NOW IN ANCIENT TIMES, THE OLDEST SON IN THE FAMILY HAD A "BIRTHRIGHT" TO INHERIT ALL HIS FATHER'S PROPERTY AND BECOME HEAD OF THE FAMILY-ESAU OWNS THAT "BIRTHRIGHT" BUT NOW JACOB THINKS HE CAN GET IT AWAY FROM HIM~

IF YOU WANT FOOD SO MUCH, GIVE ME YOUR BIRTHRIGHT!

TAKE IT! – WHAT GOOD IS IT TO ME IF I STARVE TO DEATH?

MEANWHILE, FAMINE CAME ON THE LAND – ISAAC SEEKING FOOD, SET OUT TO VISIT ABIMELECH, KING OF THE PHILISTINES IN GERAR

GOOD-BYE, DEAR HUSBAND!

KING ABIMELECH IS A PHILISTINE – DON'T TRUST HIM, FATHER!

GOOD-BYE, FATHER!

ON THE ROAD, ISAAC WONDERS WHETHER TO GO TO EGYPT INSTEAD, BUT IS ANSWERED BY A VOICE FROM HEAVEN ~

STAY IN GERAR, ISAAC, AND I WILL BLESS YOU AND WILL GIVE THESE LANDS TO YOU AND YOUR SONS – AND THEY SHALL BE FOUNDERS OF GREAT NATIONS ~ THIS PROMISE I MADE TO YOUR ANCESTOR ABRAHAM ~~ AND NOW MAKE TO YOU AND YOUR CHILDREN

SO ISAAC OBEYED GOD. HE REMAINED IN GERAR AND PROSPERED WITH GOD'S AID. BUT SOME PHILISTINES ENVIED HIM ~

HOW IS IT THAT THIS STRANGER IS SO PROSPEROUS WHILE WE PHILISTINES ARE STILL POOR!

WE'LL FIX HIM!

OUT OF SPITE, THE PHILISTINES FILLED THE WELLS WHERE ISAAC'S FLOCKS AND HERDS DRANK ~~~

THEY HAVE FILLED THE WELL!

WHO DID THIS? THE FLOCKS WILL DIE OF THIRST!

MUST BE THE PHILISTINES – THEY HATE FATHER!

ABIMELECH, KING OF THE PHILISTINES, HEARS THE NEWS AND SENDS FOR ISAAC ~

I WARN YOU, ISAAC. TAKE YOUR FAMILY AND LEAVE – MY PEOPLE HATE YOU – YOU ARE NOT SAFE HERE!

I'VE DONE NOTHING! – BUT I'LL TAKE MY FAMILY OUT OF DANGER!

SO AFTER ALL HIS HARD WORK, ISAAC HAD TO BREAK UP HIS HOME IN GERAR AND LOOK FOR A NEW PLACE TO LIVE ~

I HATE THIS PLACE!

WE SHALL MAKE A NEW HOME AND BEGIN AGAIN, WHERE GOD DIRECTS!

LATER

WE SHALL DIG A WELL, AND MAKE A NEW HOME HERE!

THIS WOULD BE A GOOD LAND FOR FARMING

AND THERE MUST BE DEER IN THOSE WOODS!

SO ISAAC AND HIS FAMILY SETTLED DOWN A SECOND TIME - BUT DISASTER WAS TO COME AGAIN - ONE DAY...

SEE, FATHER! - THE PHILISTINES - THAT MEANS TROUBLE!

ISAAC, HIS FAMILY AND SERVANTS FOUGHT WITH THE PHILISTINES, WHO WANTED TO TAKE THE WELL AWAY FROM THEM - AND ISAAC LOST~

WE'VE GOT RID OF ISAAC AND HIS FAMILY THIS TIME!

ONCE MORE WE MUST FIND A HOME - BUT COURAGE, SONS!

FOUR TIMES ISAAC LED HIS FAMILY TO A NEW SPOT, SETTLED DOWN AND DUG A WELL. EACH TIME THE PHILISTINES CAPTURED THE WELL, AND DROVE THEM OUT...

WILL WE EVER FIND A HOME?

DON'T COMPLAIN, SON - GOD HAS MADE US A PROMISE. HE'LL NOT FORGET US!

FINALLY IN A PLACE CALLED REHOBOTH, ISAAC FOUND A HOME, AND NOW KING ABIMELECH VISITS ISAAC TO MAKE PEACE~

YOU DROVE ME AWAY - WHY DO YOU COME TO ME NOW?

WE HAVE SEEN THAT THE LORD IS WITH YOU SO LET US SIGN A COVENANT OF PEACE!

IN GRATITUDE ISAAC BUILT AN ALTAR TO GOD~

THE LORD HAS MADE ROOM FOR US AND WE SHALL BE FRUITFUL IN THE LAND!

FEAR NOT, FOR I AM WITH YOU AND WILL BLESS YOU!

YEARS PASSED AND ISAAC GREW OLD AND HALF-BLIND~

COME CLOSER, I CAN'T SEE YOU—IS THIS MY SON ESAU?

YES, FATHER, IT'S ESAU!

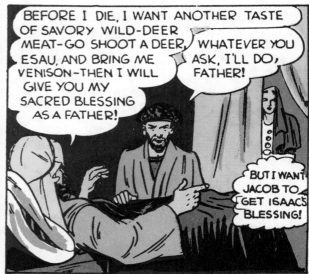

BEFORE I DIE, I WANT ANOTHER TASTE OF SAVORY WILD-DEER MEAT—GO SHOOT A DEER, ESAU, AND BRING ME VENISON—THEN I WILL GIVE YOU MY SACRED BLESSING AS A FATHER!

WHATEVER YOU ASK, I'LL DO, FATHER!

BUT I WANT JACOB TO GET ISAAC'S BLESSING!

DO AS I SAY, AND YOU'LL GET YOUR FATHER'S BLESSING INSTEAD OF ESAU—GO KILL ME TWO GOATS' KIDS FROM THE FLOCK—HURRY!

BUT ESAU IS HAIRY AND I'M SMOOTH SKINNED—IF MY FATHER FEELS ME HE'LL KNOW I'M DECEIVING HIM!

NEVER MIND!—I'LL DRESS YOU IN ESAU'S CLOTHES AND PUT THE SKINS OF THE GOATS ON YOUR HANDS—HE'LL THINK YOU'RE ESAU!

I HAVE ESAU'S BIRTHRIGHT—WHY SHOULDN'T I GET MY FATHER'S BLESSING, TOO?

WHEN THE SAVORY KID-MEAT WAS READY JACOB CARRIED IT TO HIS FATHER ISAAC—WEARING HAIRY STRIPS OF GOAT SKINS ON HIS HANDS, ARMS AND NECK~

HERE'S VENISON, FATHER—EAT, THEN BLESS ME!

IS THIS REALLY MY SON ESAU? LET ME FEEL YOU, TO MAKE SURE!

YOUR HANDS ARE THE HAIRY HANDS OF ESAU, BUT YOUR VOICE IS THE VOICE OF JACOB—ARE YOU REALLY ESAU?

I AM, FATHER, NOW GIVE ME YOUR BLESSING!

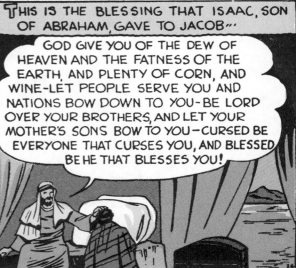

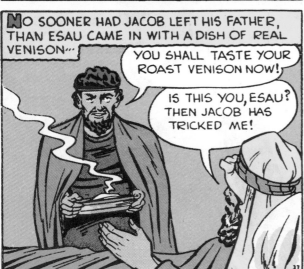

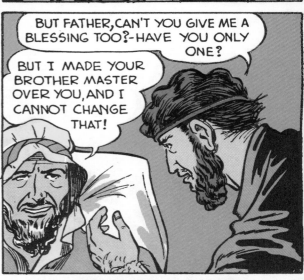

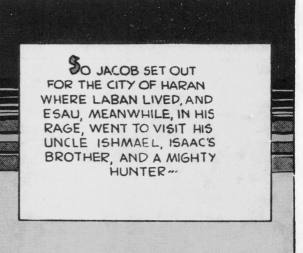

ON HIS WAY TO HIS UNCLE IN HARAN, JACOB STOPPED FOR THE NIGHT TO REST IN AN OPEN PLACE...

I AM LONELY AND AFRAID, BUT I'LL SLEEP HERE -THESE STONES WILL DO FOR A PILLOW!

DURING THE NIGHT, WHILE JACOB SLEPT HE HAD A MARVELOUS DREAM...

I AM THE LORD GOD OF ABRAHAM AND ISAAC! THROUGH YOU, ALL THE FAMILIES OF THE EARTH SHALL BE BLESSED~AND I AM WITH YOU AND WILL KEEP YOU SAFE WHEREVER YOU GO!

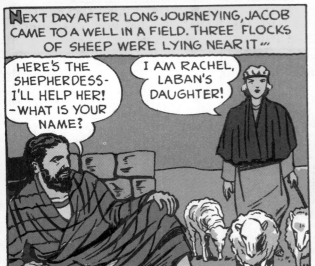

NEXT DAY AFTER LONG JOURNEYING, JACOB CAME TO A WELL IN A FIELD. THREE FLOCKS OF SHEEP WERE LYING NEAR IT...

HERE'S THE SHEPHERDESS- I'LL HELP HER! -WHAT IS YOUR NAME?

I AM RACHEL, LABAN'S DAUGHTER!

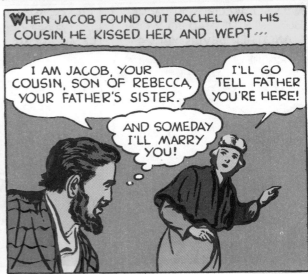

WHEN JACOB FOUND OUT RACHEL WAS HIS COUSIN, HE KISSED HER AND WEPT...

I AM JACOB, YOUR COUSIN, SON OF REBECCA, YOUR FATHER'S SISTER.

AND SOMEDAY I'LL MARRY YOU!

I'LL GO TELL FATHER YOU'RE HERE!

JACOB'S UNCLE, LABAN, PERSUADES HIM TO STAY...

YOU ARE MY KINSMAN-STAY AND WORK FOR ME AND I'LL PAY YOU WAGES!

I'LL WORK FOR YOU SEVEN YEARS FOR NOTHING IF YOU GIVE ME RACHEL FOR MY WIFE!

BUT RACHEL'S OLDER SISTER, LEAH, ALSO FALLS IN LOVE WITH JACOB...

LEAH, HOW DO YOU LIKE OUR NEW COUSIN?

I HOPE HE'LL STAY WITH US, RACHEL!

JACOB'S SEVEN YEARS SEEMED BUT A FEW DAYS, FOR THE LOVE HE BORE RACHEL WAS GREAT, FINALLY, THE WEDDING DAY!

AT LAST YOU'RE MINE!

DEAR JACOB! WILL YOU BE VERY ANGRY?

BUT THE VEILED BRIDE WAS NOT RACHEL, BUT LEAH—

WHAT!—THEY'VE DECEIVED ME! YOU'RE LEAH!

YES, BUT JACOB I LOVE YOU. —PLEASE!

JACOB RACES BACK TO LABAN—

BUT I WORKED SEVEN YEARS FOR RACHEL!

IT IS THE CUSTOM THAT THE OLDER SISTER MARRY FIRST—NOW, YOU MAY MARRY RACHEL, TOO!

AND SO JACOB WON RACHEL BUT THEN HE HAD TO WORK ANOTHER SEVEN YEARS—

RACHEL! AT LAST!

JACOB BELOVED!

YEARS WENT BY AND JACOB DECIDED TO TAKE HIS FAMILY HOME TO HIS PARENTS

IT WILL BE GOOD TO SEE THE FIELDS I USED TO PLAY AND WORK IN!

—BUT ONE THING TROUBLED JACOB—THE WRONG HE HAD DONE TO ESAU—

DRIVE THIS HERD ON AHEAD TO ESAU FOR A GIFT—AND SO EACH DAY ANOTHER HERD—I HAVE MUCH TO MAKE UP TO MY BROTHER!

AND JACOB PRAYED THAT ESAU SHOULD NOT BE ANGRY —ONCE ALL NIGHT LONG HE WRESTLED WITH A MAN HE COULD NOT SEE—

I WILL NOT LET YOU GO UNTIL YOU BLESS ME!

YOUR NAME SHALL BE NOT JACOB, BUT ISRAEL—THAT MEANS WRESTLER— WRESTLER WITH GOD!

AND THUS THE CHILDREN OF ISRAEL RECEIVED THEIR NAME

SO JACOB CAME TO ESAU, AND BOWED HIMSELF TO THE GROUND SEVEN TIMES, NOT KNOWING HOW ESAU WOULD RECEIVE HIM—

WHEN I WRESTLED WITH GOD I WAS NOT AFRAID —BUT I FEAR ESAU BECAUSE I WRONGED HIM!

JACOB

BUT ESAU FELL ON JACOB'S NECK AND THEY WEPT...

YOU DON'T HATE ME, ESAU, FOR WHAT I DID TO YOU?

NO, JACOB, THAT'S PAST AND FOR- GOTTEN! NOW SHOW ME YOUR FAMILY SO I MAY WELCOME THEM!

--AND JACOB HAD TWELVE SONS—AMONG THEM JOSEPH

The Bible Story of JOSEPH IN EGYPT

FROM THE BOOK OF GENESIS,
CHAPTERS 37 THROUGH 41

PART ONE

JACOB, WHO DWELT IN CANAAN, HAD TWELVE SONS.

YOU ARE MY BELOVED, JOSEPH, MY FAVORITE AND SON OF MY OLD AGE!

FATHER, WILL YOU MAKE ME THE COAT OF MANY COLORS AS YOU PROMISED?

LAST NIGHT I DREAMED WE WERE BINDING SHEAVES. MY SHEAVES AROSE, WHILE MY BROTHERS' BOWED TO MINE!

I DREAMED AGAIN, FATHER-THE SUN, MOON AND ELEVEN STARS BOWED TO ME.

HMPH!

WHAT IS THIS DREAM— SHALL WE ALL INDEED BOW TO YOU, JOSEPH?

THE BROTHERS WENT TO FEED THEIR FLOCKS AND TALK OF JOSEPH---

LET'S GET RID OF HIM!

PUT HIM FOREVER OUT OF THE WAY!

THERE THEY GO!

NOW TAKE JOSEPH'S COAT AND DRAW GOAT'S BLOOD AND DIP THE COAT INTO IT— OUR FATHER WILL THINK JOSEPH HAS BEEN ATTACKED!

LATER—BACK AT HOME

WE HAVE FOUND THIS COAT! IS IT NOT JOSEPH'S COAT?

JACOB IS SHAKEN WITH GRIEF

IT IS MY SON'S COAT— AN EVIL BEAST HAS DEVOURED HIM—JOSEPH IS WITHOUT DOUBT RENT IN PIECES!

NEARING EGYPT

WE SHALL SELL YOU FOR A PROFIT IN EGYPT, ISRAELITE!

THEY CAME AT LAST TO EGYPT AND MET POTIPHAR, CAPTAIN OF PHARAOH'S GUARD ---

HE'S A HEALTHY LAD— I'LL BUY HIM!

POTIPHAR TAKES JOSEPH TO THE FIELDS

DO WELL, ISRAELITE, AND YOU SHALL BE ADVANCED!

I SHALL FORGET MY ANGER AND WIN FAVOR HERE!

As TIME PASSED, THE LORD WAS WITH JOSEPH AND POTIPHAR SAW THAT THE LORD MADE ALL THAT HE DID PROSPER—

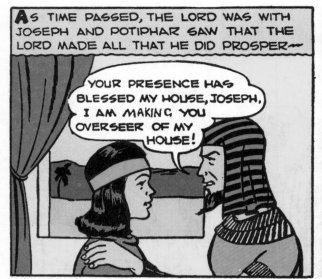

YOUR PRESENCE HAS BLESSED MY HOUSE, JOSEPH, I AM MAKING YOU OVERSEER OF MY HOUSE!

AND THE LORD BLESSED THE EGYPTIAN'S HOUSE FOR JOSEPH'S SAKE AND THE BLESSING WAS ON ALL THAT HE HAD IN THE HOUSE AND IN THE FIELD—

JOSEPH GREW INTO A HANDSOME MAN AND POTIPHAR'S WIFE ATTEMPTED TO GAIN HIS AFFECTION—

BUT JOSEPH WAS ALOOF BECAUSE HE KNEW POTIPHAR WOULD NOT LIKE HIS FRIENDSHIP WITH THE WOMEN—

POTIPHAR'S WIFE LIES TO HIM TO GET JOSEPH INTO TROUBLE—

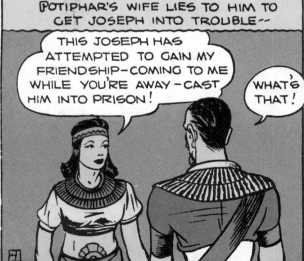

THIS JOSEPH HAS ATTEMPTED TO GAIN MY FRIENDSHIP—COMING TO ME WHILE YOU'RE AWAY—CAST HIM INTO PRISON!

WHAT'S THAT!

GUARD, SEIZE THIS JOSEPH AND THROW HIM INTO PRISON ON MY COMMAND!

ANOTHER PRISONER, KEEPER!

THINGS GO WRONG SO OFTEN! I AM JUST—BUT AM I PUNISHED—YET MUST I BE FIRM AND GOOD!

AS TIME PASSED THE LORD BLESSED JOSEPH IN PRISON—HE WAS MADE ASSISTANT TO THE JAILOR ~~~~

SINCE YOU'VE BEEN HERE WE'VE ALL BEEN BLESSED—I'M PLACING THE PRISONERS IN YOUR CARE!

LATER ~~~

WHY ARE YOU SO SAD?

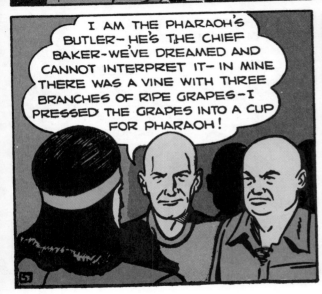

I AM THE PHARAOH'S BUTLER—HE'S THE CHIEF BAKER—WE'VE DREAMED AND CANNOT INTERPRET IT—IN MINE THERE WAS A VINE WITH THREE BRANCHES OF RIPE GRAPES—I PRESSED THE GRAPES INTO A CUP FOR PHARAOH!

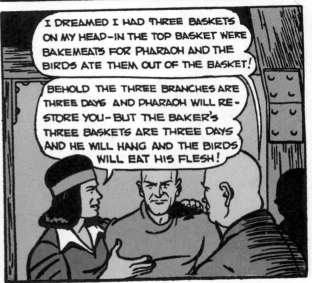

I DREAMED I HAD THREE BASKETS ON MY HEAD—IN THE TOP BASKET WERE BAKEMEATS FOR PHARAOH AND THE BIRDS ATE THEM OUT OF THE BASKET!

BEHOLD THE THREE BRANCHES ARE THREE DAYS AND PHARAOH WILL RE-STORE YOU—BUT THE BAKER'S THREE BASKETS ARE THREE DAYS AND HE WILL HANG AND THE BIRDS WILL EAT HIS FLESH!

CAN JOSEPH INTERPRET DREAMS RIGHTLY?

HA! WE SHALL SEE!

BEHOLD, AS JOSEPH INTERPRETED, IN THREE DAYS THE BUTLER WAS RESTORED AND SERVED THE KING BUT THE BAKER WAS HANGED TO A TREE

FRESH GRAPE JUICE FOR YOUR TABLE, OH MIGHTY PHARAOH!

LATER PHARAOH BECOMES WORRIED

I HAVE HAD DREAMS LATELY— —BUT WILL I SLEEP TONIGHT?

PHARAOH DID NOT SLEEP—BUT DREAMED~~

THERE!—SEVEN FAT CATTLE CAME OUT OF A RIVER — SEVEN LEAN ONES RUNNING UP TO DEVOUR THE FAT!— WHAT'S IT MEAN?

STILL LATER

ANOTHER NIGHT— ANOTHER DREAM!

CAN WE HEAR YOUR DREAMS, SIRE?

ANOTHER DREAM—SEVEN GOOD EARS OF CORN GREW UP AND SEVEN LEAN EARS CAME AND DEVOURED THE GOOD ONES!

STRANGE! YOUR SERVANTS ARE UNABLE TO INTERPRET THE DREAMS!

THE BUTLER SEEKS AN AUDIENCE WITH PHARAOH~

I HAD FORGOTTEN! —A MAN LIES IN THE DUNGEONS WHO CAN TELL OF DREAMS —PHARAOH SHOULD HEAR HIM!

SEND FOR THIS ISRAELITE NAMED JOSEPH—IF HE INTERPRETED YOUR DREAMS HE SHALL MINE!

THEN PHARAOH SENDS TO THE PRISON FOR JOSEPH

GOOD NEWS FOR YOU, JOSEPH—PHARAOH HAS SENT FOR YOU TO INTERPRET HIS DREAMS!

JOSEPH STANDS BEFORE PHARAOH~

THERE IS NONE THAT CAN INTERPRET MY DREAM BUT I HAVE HEARD THAT YOU CAN UNDERSTAND A DREAM TO INTERPRET IT!

THE DREAM IS TOLD TO JOSEPH~

IT IS NOT IN ME—GOD SHALL GIVE PHARAOH AN ANSWER~ THE TWO DREAMS ARE ONE. GOD HAS SHOWED PHARAOH WHAT HE IS ABOUT TO DO— THE SEVEN GOOD CATTLE ARE SEVEN YEARS AND THE SEVEN GOOD EARS ARE SEVEN YEARS OF PLENTY!

HMM!

THE SEVEN THIN CATTLE AND SEVEN THIN EARS ARE SEVEN YEARS OF FAMINE—NOW LET PHARAOH PICK A MAN DISCREET AND WISE, AND SET HIM OVER THE LAND OF EGYPT—LET HIM GATHER ALL THE FOOD OF THE GOOD YEARS!

THE IDEA IS GOOD!

⑦

CAN WE FIND SUCH A MAN AS THIS IS, A MAN IN WHOM THE SPIRIT OF GOD IS? FOR AS MUCH AS GOD HATH SHOWED YOU ALL THIS, THERE IS NONE SO DISCREET AND WISE AS YOU ARE! YOU SHALL BE PLACED OVER THE LAND AND SHALL BE SECOND ONLY TO ME

The Story of JOSEPH IN EGYPT

PART TWO

FROM THE BOOK OF GENESIS, CHAPTERS 41 THROUGH 50.

JOSEPH—HAVING BEEN SOLD INTO SLAVERY IN EGYPT BY HIS JEALOUS BROTHERS BECOMES RULER NEXT TO PHARAOH WHEN HE ALONE CAN INTERPRET THE KING'S PROPHETIC DREAMS

IF MY PROPHECIES ARE TRUE WE SHALL HAVE PLENTY AT THE END OF THE SEVEN YEARS OF PLENTY!

SEVEN YEARS AFTER---

THE FAMINE HAS COME AS JOSEPH HAS PROPHESIED!

AND WHEN ALL THE LAND OF EGYPT WAS FAMISHED THE PEOPLE CRIED FOR FOOD

GO TO JOSEPH HE WILL SELL YOU FOOD!

OPEN THE STOREHOUSE AND DISTRIBUTE FOOD TO ALL!

ONLY IN EGYPT WAS FOOD PLENTY AND EVEN ISRAEL SUFFERED FROM THE WIDESPREAD FAMINE ~~~

GO TO EGYPT AND BUY US FOOD!

WE OBEY!

BUT MY BELOVED YOUNGEST SON, BENJAMIN REMAINS WITH ME!

JOSEPH'S BROTHERS WENT TO EGYPT ~~~

THE BROTHERS ARRIVE BEFORE JOSEPH BUT DON'T RECOGNIZE HIM ~~~

YOU COME FROM CANAAN?

BUT JOSEPH KNEW THEM ~~~

YOU ARE SPIES THAT HAVE COME TO SEE THE NAKEDNESS OF THE LAND!

I KNOW MY BROTHERS - THEY KNOW ME NOT!

WE ARE NOT SPIES - BUT SONS OF JACOB IN CANAAN - THE YOUNGEST IS WITH OUR FATHER AND ONE IS DEAD!

YOU SHALL PROVE YOU ARE NOT SPIES! - I SHALL HOLD ONE OF YOU IN PRISON UNTIL YOU FETCH YOUR YOUNGEST BROTHER SO I MAY SEE HIM!

SO SIMEON IS BOUND AND SENT TO PRISON

TRULY - GOVERNOR JOSEPH IS A HARSH MAN!

LATER ~~~

FILL THE SACKS WITH GRAIN — RESTORE THEIR MONEY — HASTEN!

THE BROTHERS STOP ENROUTE AT AN INN AND MAKE A DISCOVERY ~~~

LOOK! MY MONEY IS RESTORED HERE!

ALL OUR MONEY IS RESTORED! — THE GOVERNOR HAS BEEN KIND!

AFTER DAYS, THEY ARRIVE AT HOME ~~

THE GOVERNOR TOOK US TO BE SPIES!

WE MUST BRING BACK BENJAMIN!

SIMEON IS HELD AS HOSTAGE UNTIL WE DO!

LATER — THEY NEED FOOD AGAIN ~~~

YOU SAY ONLY TAKING BENJAMIN BACK WILL PROVE YOU NOT TO BE SPIES? — I FEAR EVIL, MY SONS!

SIMEON WILL SUFFER UNLESS WE RETURN!

LISTEN TO OUR PLEA, FATHER!

SO BE IT! WE MUST HAVE FOOD — TAKE PRESENTS OF HONEY, BALM AND SPICES!

I SHALL BE SURETY, FATHER, AND TAKE THE BLAME IF HARM COMES TO BENJAMIN!

SOMETIME LATER THE BROTHERS RETURN TO EGYPT ~~~

MY BROTHERS DO RETURN! BRING THEM TO DINNER WITH ME AT NOON!

WE RETURN AS PROMISED! BUT MUST HAVE FOOD — WE ALSO RETURN THE MONEY FOUND IN OUR SACKS WHEN WE LEFT!

PEACE BE TO YOU I PUT THE MONEY THERE!

AT NOON THEY WERE TAKEN BEFORE JOSEPH ~~

WE BRING GIFTS FROM JACOB, OUR FATHER!

THANK YOU— COME AND DINE!

FILL THEIR SACKS AGAIN WITH FOOD— BUT PUT MY SILVER CUP IN BENJAMIN'S SACK!

AFTERWARD THE BROTHERS TAKE LEAVE

NOW!—FOLLOW THEM—FIND MY CUP!

SO GUARDS STOPPED THE CARAVAN ~~

BUT HOW? OUR YOUNGEST WOULD NOT STEAL!

THAT I WOULD NOT— I DID NOT!

IT'S THE GOVERNOR'S CUP!

THEY ARE LED BACK TO JOSEPH ~~

WHAT SHALL WE DO NOW?

WE ARE INNOCENT— GOD WILL AID US!

ONE BROTHER SPEAKS UP BEFORE JOSEPH

OH, MY LORD—I HAVE PROMISED TO BE SURETY FOR MY BROTHER—HOLD ME IN BONDAGE BUT LET BENJAMIN GO HOME OR HIS FATHER WILL DIE OF GRIEF!

HOW SHALL I GO BACK TO MY FATHER AND THE LAD BE NOT WITH ME? WHEN HE SEES THAT THE LAD IS NOT WITH US HE WILL DIE WITH SORROW!—HOLD ME AND LET THE LAD GO HOME WITH HIS BROTHERS!

WHAT IS IT?—THE GOVERNOR WEEPS!

PRAY SIR—WHAT HAVE WE DONE?

DON'T YOU KNOW ME?—I AM JOSEPH YOUR BROTHER WHOM YOU SOLD INTO EGYPT!—BE NOT GRIEVED NOR ANGRY WITH YOURSELVES THAT YOU SOLD ME HERE—FOR GOD SENT ME BEFORE YOU TO PRESERVE LIFE!

—SO IT WAS NOT YOU THAT SENT ME HERE BUT GOD HAS DONE IT!—NOW GO AND BRING MY FATHER HERE FOR THERE IS YET FIVE YEARS OF FAMINE—YOU SHALL DWELL IN THE LAND OF GOSHEN AND SHALL BE NEAR ME!

I SHALL BRING YOU BEFORE PHARAOH!—HE SHALL WELCOME YOU—AND OUR FATHER!

ONCE MORE THE BROTHERS GO BACK TO CANAAN ~~~

WE SHALL FIND PLENTY AND JOY IN EGYPT!

AND WE HAD NOT RECOGNISED JOSEPH!

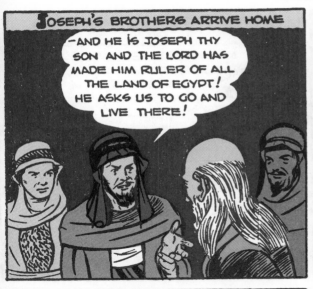

JOSEPH'S BROTHERS ARRIVE HOME

—AND HE IS JOSEPH THY SON AND THE LORD HAS MADE HIM RULER OF ALL THE LAND OF EGYPT! HE ASKS US TO GO AND LIVE THERE!

I DEPART SADLY BUT THERE IS JOY WITHIN ME FOR I SHALL SEE JOSEPH!

COME—WE SHALL GO!

WHEN JACOB SEES JOSEPH HE WEEPS WITH JOY—

FATHER, YOU HAVE COME!

JOSEPH—MY SON—WHOM I THOUGHT DEAD ALL THESE YEARS! GOD IS GOOD TO ME!

JOSEPH TAKES HIS FATHER BEFORE PHARAOH—

THE LAND OF EGYPT IS BEFORE THEE. YOU SHALL DWELL IN THE BEST OF THE LAND!

MAY GOD BLESS YOU, OH PHARAOH!

THE FAMINE GREW WORSE AND THE PEOPLE OF EGYPT FAINTED FROM HUNGER—

WE HAVE NO MORE MONEY TO BUY FOOD, MASTER, GIVE US FOOD OR WE DIE!

GIVE YOUR CATTLE FOR FOOD!

AS THE YEARS OF FAMINE WENT BY THE PEOPLE OF EGYPT HAD NO MONEY TO PAY FOR FOOD SO JOSEPH HAD THEM EXCHANGE THEIR CATTLE AND LATER THEIR LAND FOR FOOD. HE THEN GAVE THEM SEED TO GROW ON THEIR LAND, GIVING THE FIFTH PART OF THE INCREASE TO PHARAOH AS NOW THE PEOPLE WERE UNDER BONDAGE TO HIM—PHARAOH WAS A KIND RULER. AND THE PEOPLE LOVED HIM—

ONLY IN EGYPT WAS THERE FOOD

I HAVE BROUGHT HAPPINESS TO ALL! —GOD HAS BEEN GOOD TO US!

JOSEPH TAKES HIS SONS TO SEE JACOB ~~~

I AM DYING, JOSEPH, MY SON— BUT BEFORE I GO I WILL BLESS THY TWO SONS!

JACOB DIED AND THE BROTHERS CAME TO JOSEPH ~~~

WILT THOU PUNISH US NOW THAT JACOB IS GONE?

FEAR NOT FOR I HAVE FORGIVEN EVERYONE!

THE FAMINE ENDED AT LAST, AND PLENTY RETURNED ~~~

JOSEPH SAVED US!

WE CAN CARRY ON NOW, JOSEPH!

I GROW OLD, BROTHERS— SOON I SHALL FOLLOW OUR FATHER JACOB!

WE ARE ALL OLD, JOSEPH, BUT YOU'VE BEEN GOOD! YOUR NAME SHALL BE REMEMBERED!

I HAVE LIVED 100 AND 10 YEARS, MY TIME HAS COME!

YOU SHALL BE BURIED IN SPLENDOR, JOSEPH, FOR ALL EGYPT AS WELL AS WE LOVE YOU!

THE END

The Story of MOSES AND HIS STRUGGLE FOR ISRAEL

PART ONE — OUT OF EGYPT

FROM THE BOOKS OF GENESIS, EXODUS AND NUMBERS.

BEHOLD THE CHILDREN OF ISRAEL ARE MORE AND MIGHTIER THEN WE! — LET US GET CONTROL OVER THEM SO THEY CANNOT OVER-RUN US OR JOIN OUR ENEMIES!

SO PHARAOH PUT TASKMASTERS OVER THE HEBREWS AND SET THEM AT HARD TASKS MAKING THEIR LIVES BITTER UNDER THIS CRUEL BONDAGE ~~

SLAVE — YOU'LL WORK 'TILL YOU DROP!

AFFLICTION DID NOT DOWN THE ISRAELITES, SO PHARAOH MADE A DECREE

ALL HEBREW SONS NEW-BORN WILL BE CAST INTO THE RIVER — ONLY THE DAUGHTERS SHALL BE SAVED!

NOW A HEBREW WOMAN BORE A SON AND HID HIM THREE MONTHS —

WE CAN'T HIDE HIM HERE ANY LONGER, MOTHER, LET US FIND A SAFE PLACE!

THE MOTHER AND DAUGHTER HID THE BABY AT THE RIVER'S BRINK ~~~

NOW HE SHALL LIVE!

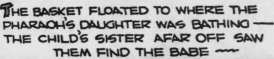

THE BASKET FLOATED TO WHERE THE PHARAOH'S DAUGHTER WAS BATHING — THE CHILD'S SISTER AFAR OFF SAW THEM FIND THE BABE —

THE CHILD'S SISTER HAS AN IDEA AND APPROACHES THE PRINCESS —

I SAW FROM AFAR AND CAME TO ASK IF I MAY CALL A NURSE FOR THEE?

IF THOU KNOWEST ONE, GO!

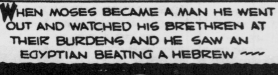

THE DAUGHTER BRINGS THE CHILD'S OWN MOTHER BEFORE THE PRINCESS —

NURSE THIS CHILD, TAKE CARE OF IT AND I'LL PAY YOU WELL!

THE LITTLE MOSES GREW TO A BOY AND PHARAOH'S DAUGHTER CALLED HIM HER OWN SON —

MY SON, YOU GROW FAST!

WHEN MOSES BECAME A MAN HE WENT OUT AND WATCHED HIS BRETHREN AT THEIR BURDENS AND HE SAW AN EGYPTIAN BEATING A HEBREW —

VILE ONE!

ENRAGED AT SUCH CRUELTY TO HIS RACE, MOSES KILLED THE EGYPTIAN —

THIS FOR TYRANNY!

MOSES FLED SWIFTLY, KNOWING WELL PHARAOH WOULD SEEK TO PUNISH HIM.

HE CAME TO THE LAND OF MIDIAN AND RESTED BY A WELL ~~~

SO FAR I'M FREE — THIS WATER REFRESHES!

IN MIDIAN, ITS PRIEST HAD SEVEN DAUGHTERS WHO CAME TO THIS WELL TO WATER THEIR FATHER'S FLOCK— BUT SOME SHEPHERDS DROVE THEM OFF

GO! NO INTERFERENCE!

MOSES STOOD UP TO AID THE DAUGHTERS — THE SHEPHERDS GAVE WAY ~~~

WE MUST REPAY THIS MAN!

FOR ILL-TREATING WOMEN, YOU BULLIES!

MOSES IS LED TO THE PRIEST BY HIS DAUGHTERS ~~~

THIS EGYPTIAN SAVED US FROM THE ROUGH SHEPHERDS AND HELPED US WATER THE FLOCK!

FINE—HE CAN STAY WITH US!

MOSES STAYED AND LATER MARRIED ONE OF THE DAUGHTERS AND THEY HAD A SON NAMED GERSHOM ~~~

AND IT CAME TO PASS IN THE PROCESS OF TIME, PHARAOH DIED AND THE CHILDREN OF ISRAEL CRIED TO GOD IN THEIR BONDAGE TO RELIEVE THEM ～～

ONE DAY WHEN MOSES WAS WATCHING THE FLOCK THE LORD APPEARED TO HIM IN A FLAMING BUSH ～～

I AM THE GOD OF THY FATHER, THE GOD OF ABRAHAM, THE GOD OF ISAAC, AND THE GOD OF JACOB! - I AM SENDING THEE TO EGYPT TO DELIVER MY PEOPLE!

I WILL DELIVER YOUR PEOPLE FROM THE EGYPTIANS—THEY SHALL GO TO A LAND OF MILK AND HONEY! GET THY BROTHER AARON WHO SHALL BE SPOKESMAN AND YOUR ROD SHALL DO MIRACLES IN MY NAME!

MOSES TOOK HIS WIFE AND SONS, TO MEET AARON, AND PREPARE TO LEAVE ～～

A GRAVE TASK! BUT I GO TO DO GOD'S WILL!

SO AARON BECAME SPOKESMAN AND TALKED TO THE ISRAELITES ～～

THE LORD HATH SENT MOSES TO DELIVER US OUT OF THE LAND OF EGYPT!

MOSES AND AARON SEEK PHARAOH TOGETHER ~~~

THE LORD GOD SAYS LET MY PEOPLE GO THAT THEY MAY HOLD A FEAST UNTO HIM IN THE WILDERNESS!

WHO IS THE LORD THAT I SHOULD OBEY HIS VOICE TO LET ISRAEL GO?

I KNOW NOT THE LORD, NEITHER WILL I LET ISRAEL GO!—MAYBE THE PEOPLE DO NOT HAVE ENOUGH WORK WHEN THEY WANT TO FEAST!

SO PHARAOH CALLS HIS TASK-MASTERS

LET MORE WORK BE UPON ISRAEL— GIVE THEM NO MORE STRAW TO MAKE BRICK BUT LET THEM GET STRAW THEMSELVES!

FINALLY THE ISRAELITE LEADERS COMPLAINED TO MOSES AND AARON OF THE NEW TASKS ~~~

INSTEAD OF DELIVERING US OUT OF EGYPT YOU HAVE CAUSED OUR SLAVERY TO BECOME GREATER!

ASKING GOD FOR HELP, MOSES RECEIVES HIS ANSWER

NOW SHALT THOU SEE WHAT I WILL DO TO PHARAOH —I WILL MAKE THEE A GOD TO PHARAOH AND AARON SHALL BE THY PROPHET!

MOSES AND AARON ONCE MORE VISIT PHARAOH ~~~

THE LORD ASKS THEE AGAIN, PHARAOH TO LET HIS PEOPLE GO!

SHOW ME A MIRACLE!

To PROVE GOD WAS WITH THEM MOSES TOLD AARON TO CAST HIS ROD BEFORE PHARAOH – THE ROD TURNED INTO A SNAKE!

STILL PHARAOH WOULD NOT LET ISRAEL GO AND THUS MOSES AND AARON TURNED THE RIVER TO BLOOD–

THIS MAN MOSES MUST TRULY BE A GOD HIMSELF!

PHARAOH'S HEART REMAINED HARD UNTIL MOSES BROUGHT A PLAGUE OF FROGS, AT GOD'S WORD, ON EGYPT–

UGH! – HUNDREDS OF THEM!

FINALLY PHARAOH PROMISED TO LET ISRAEL GO, AND THE FROG PLAGUE ENDED – BUT –

HMM–THINGS ARE ALLRIGHT NOW! – THEY ARE VERY USEFUL! – I CHANGE MY MIND – THEY SHALL NOT GO!

So GOD COMMANDED MOSES AND AARON TO MAKE A PLAGUE OF LICE AND FLIES–

THEY'RE EVERYWHERE!

THIS WAS TOO MUCH FOR PHARAOH SO HE CALLED FOR MOSES AND AARON AND TOLD THEM TO CALL OFF THE FLIES AND HE WOULD LET THE PEOPLE GO AND SERVE THEIR GOD. –WHEN THE FLIES WERE GONE HE CHANGED HIS MIND AGAIN SO THE LORD KILLED ALL THE CATTLE OF EGYPT AND SENT A PLAGUE OF BOILS AND HAILSTORMS ON ALL THE EGYPTIANS.

THEN A PLAGUE OF LOCUSTS CAME WITH THE EAST WIND BUT PHARAOH WAS STILL HARDENED SO THE LORD HAD MOSES CAUSE DARKNESS TO COME ON THE LAND ~~

THREE DAYS AND NO LIGHT!

PHARAOH'S PROMISES ARE WORTHLESS — HE STILL CHANGES HIS MIND ~~

NO! — I WILL NOT LET THEM GO! NOW GET OUT OF MY SIGHT!

GOD WILL SEND ANOTHER PLAGUE!

MOSES CALLS HIS PEOPLE TOGETHER ~~

BEHOLD — KILL A LAMB AND STRIKE THE BLOOD ON THE TWO SIDE POSTS AND UPPER DOOR POSTS OF YOUR HOUSES FOR THE LORD WILL SLAY THE FIRST BORN OF THOSE WITHOUT THE BLOOD!

AND AT MIDNIGHT THE LORD SMOTE ALL THE FIRSTBORN IN EGYPT FROM PHARAOH DOWN TO THE FIRSTBORN OF THE CAPTIVE THAT WAS IN THE DUNGEON ~~

OH PHARAOH, THY SON IS DEAD AND IT IS THE SAME THROUGHOUT THE LAND!

PHARAOH'S SERVANTS PLEAD WITH HIM ~~

OH, MIGHTY PHARAOH, IT IS BEST THAT YOU SEND ISRAEL AWAY BEFORE WE BE ALL DEAD MEN!

YES! — I WILL DO IT!

7

AT LAST PHARAOH RELENTS AND CALLS MOSES AND AARON ~~

— GET OUT FROM AMONG MY PEOPLE AND TAKE THE CHILDREN OF ISRAEL AND GO SERVE YOUR LORD AS YOU SAID!

The Story of MOSES
AND HIS STRUGGLE FOR ISRAEL

PART TWO
THE PROMISED LAND

FROM THE BOOKS OF EXODUS, LEVITICUS, NUMBERS AND DEUTERONOMY

MOSES LEADS HIS PEOPLE FROM EGYPT~

- AND THE LORD WENT BEFORE THEM BY DAY IN A PILLAR OF A CLOUD AND A PILLAR OF FIRE AT NIGHT, TO LEAD THE WAY.

THE LORD TOLD MOSES TO CAMP BETWEEN MIGDOL AND THE SEA

BUT THE HEART OF PHARAOH AGAIN GREW HARDENED~

WHY HAVE WE DONE THIS, THAT WE HAVE LET ISRAEL GO FROM SERVING US? LET US GO AFTER THEM!

YES!

WITH ALL THE ARMY AND CHARIOTS OF EGYPT, KING PHARAOH PURSUED ISRAEL

WHEN THE CHILDREN OF ISRAEL SAW THE EGYPTIANS THEY CRIED WITH FEAR~

IT IS AS WELL THAT WE DIED IN EGYPT, THAN HERE!

FEAR NOT!

THE LORD TOLD MOSES TO RAISE HIS ROD OVER THE SEA—AND IT OPENED UP!

AND THE WATERS WERE A WALL ON THEIR RIGHT AND LEFT ---

PASS THROUGH THE SEA ON DRY LAND — THE LORD WILL DELIVER YOU FROM THE EGYPTIANS!

THE EGYPTIANS PURSUED THEM INTO THE MIDST OF THE SEA ---

WE'LL CATCH ISRAEL!

MOSES COMMANDED AT GOD'S WORD, AND THE SEA RETURNED TO ITS BED!

RETURN TO WATERS, IN THE LORD'S NAME!

THE WATERS RETURNED AND COVERED PHARAOH AND HIS HOST IN THE SEA ---

MOSES BROUGHT ISRAEL FROM THE SEA AND THEY TRAVELED THREE DAYS IN THE WILDERNESS AND FOUND NO WATER ---

BUT WE NEED WATER NOW!

COMING TO MARAH, THEY FOUND WATER BUT IT WAS BITTER ---

WE CAN'T DRINK THIS, MOSES. WHAT SHALL WE DO?

THE LORD SHOWED MOSES A TREE WHICH, WHEN CAST IN THE WATER, THE WATER WAS MADE SWEET ---

SO THEY CAME TO ELIM, WHERE WERE 12 WELLS, AND CAMPED -----

HERE WE SHALL REST-BE SAFE FOR AWHILE!

LATER, THE ISRAELITES JOURNEYED ON TOWARD SINAI ---

WE NEED BREAD!

GOD WILL GIVE MOSES POWER TO GIVE US BREAD!

MOSES OVERCOMES ALL TROUBLES ---

YOU ASK FOR WATER! ROCK OF HOREB YIELDS THRU GOD'S POWER!

OUT OF THE LAND CAME THE AMALEKITES, TO STOP ISRAEL --

- I GO TO YONDER HILL— HOLD OFF THE ENEMY!

AYE, MOSES!

WHEN MOSES RAISES HIS ARM, THE AMALEKITES RETREAT — HE DROPS HIS ARM, THEY COME BACK!

AARON! HUR! MY ARM TIRES! HOLD IT UP— SO LONG AS IT'S UP, WE WIN!

COMING, MOSES!

HOURS LATER ---

THEY FLEE! ISRAEL TRIUMPHS AGAIN!

FINALLY THE ISRAELITES COME TO SINAI~

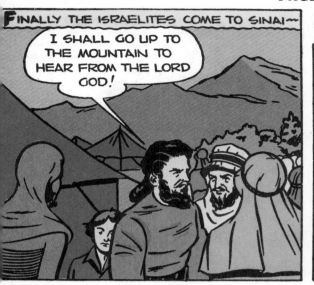

I SHALL GO UP TO THE MOUNTAIN TO HEAR FROM THE LORD GOD!

GOD SPEAKS FROM THE CLOUDS

I AM YOUR GOD! THOU SHALT HAVE NO OTHER GODS BEFORE ME!

AND SO MOSES RECEIVED THE TEN COMMANDMENTS ON THE MOUNT AND BROUGHT THEM DOWN, ON TABLETS TO ISRAEL ~~

THE WORDS OF GOD ARE HERE WRITTEN — TEN COMMANDS HE GIVES TO ALL!

THE COMMANDMENTS

1. I AM THE LORD, THY GOD. THOU SHALT HAVE NO OTHER GODS BEFORE ME.
2. THOU SHALT NOT MAKE ANY GRAVEN IMAGE.
3. THOU SHALT NOT TAKE GOD'S NAME IN VAIN.
4. REMEMBER THE SABBATH — KEEP IT HOLY
5. HONOR THY FATHER AND MOTHER
6. THOU SHALT NOT KILL
7. THOU SHALT NOT COMMIT ADULTERY
8. THOU SHALT NOT STEAL.
9. THOU SHALT NOT BEAR FALSE WITNESS.
10. THOU SHALT NOT COVET.

LATER, MOSES WENT TO THE MOUNT FOR FORTY DAYS AND NIGHTS TO LEARN OF GOD ~~

LET THE PEOPLE MAKE ME A SANCTUARY — A TABERNACLE IN WHICH I MAY DWELL AND BE WITH MY PEOPLE!

I OBEY THY WORD, OH LORD!

MOSES' DELAY IN RETURNING BROUGHT UNREST AMONG THE ISRAELITES~~

YOU WILL BE OUR LEADER, AARON!

YOU WILL BE OUR LEADER! – YOU WILL MAKE US A GOLDEN CALF TO WORSHIP!

WELL!

MOSES RETURNS IN ANGER AND BREAKS THE TABLETS~~

DANCING AND WORSHIP-PING A GOLDEN CALF! YOU GRIEVE ME, OH ISRAEL!

MOSES BURNED THE CALF, AND MADE A CHALLENGE~~

WHOEVER IS WITH ME, COME OVER! ALL OTHERS SHALL BE SLAIN!

THE TRIBE OF LEVI IS WITH YOU, MOSES!

MANY DIED THAT TIME – BUT STILL THE PEOPLE MURMURED, UNTIL THEY SAW A PILLAR OF CLOUD FROM HEAVEN ENVELOPE MOSES~~

OH LORD, SHOW ME THE RIGHT WAY TO LEAD MY FLOCK!

I RELENT AND SHALL BE WITH YOU AND GIVE REST!

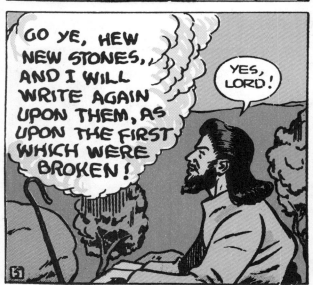

GO YE, HEW NEW STONES, AND I WILL WRITE AGAIN UPON THEM, AS UPON THE FIRST WHICH WERE BROKEN!

YES, LORD!

AND AFTERWARD, MOSES HAD THE TWO TABLETS ON THE MOUNTAINSIDE AND CAME TO HIS PEOPLE, SMILING~~

PEACE! LET US TALK AGAIN TOGETHER!

HE IS HAPPY! HIS FACE SHINES SO!

MOSES HAS A TABERNACLE ERECTED ~~

MY PEOPLE HAVE DONE AS GOD WILLED! HE SHALL BLESS THEM, ONE AND ALL!

AND SO MOSES FINISHED HIS WORK WHEN THE TABERNACLE WAS DONE AND FURNISHED, ACCORDING TO THE BOOK OF EXODUS

WE ARE HAPPY, MOSES!

YES, AARON!

SOON THE LORD GOD SPOKE AGAIN TO MOSES, NOW AT LENGTH, AND HE TOLD MOSES THE LAWS WHICH WERE TO BE MADE, AND THE CUSTOMS ESTABLISHED TO LIVE BY — AND THIS IS A PURPOSE OF THE FIVE BOOKS OF MOSES WHICH RELATES ALL THE LAWS AND ORDERS OF THE OLD HEBREWS FOR THEIR PROMISED LAND!

SO THE ISRAELITES MOVE FROM SINAI TO PARAN, AND THEY FIND A GUIDE TO TAKE THEM ~~~

HOBAB THE MIDIANITE, AID US TO SEEK OUR PROMISED LAND!

WE NEED YOU AS A GUIDE!

I WILL HELP!

LATER, THEY STOP AND REST ENROUTE ~~~

FROM HERE I SHALL NAME THOSE TO SPY OUT THE PARAN WILDERNESS AND TO FIND US A FINAL SETTLEMENT!

I SHALL GO!

AND I—

AND THEY RETURNED FROM SEARCHING, AFTER FORTY DAYS ~~~~

WE CAME UNTO A LAND SURELY FILLED WITH MILK AND HONEY!

WE MUST FIGHT MANY FOR IT!

GOD WAS WITH MOSES, AND THE ISRAELITES TRIUMPHED OVER ALL THE ENEMIES~

WE HAVE COME TO THE PLAINS OF MOAB! COUNT OUR MULTITUDE-WE'LL SOON BE ON THE SHORES OF THE JORDAN, SHOWN US AS THE PROMISED LAND!

REMEMBER OUR LAWS, YE PEOPLE! KEEP THEM ALWAYS— AND WE SHALL ALWAYS TRIUMPH!

AND THE LORD SPOKE TO MOSES AGAIN~

DEFILE NOT THE LAND ABOUT TO BE INHERITED, AND I, THE LORD YOUR GOD, SHALL DWELL THERE, AND AMONG THE CHILDREN OF ISRAEL!

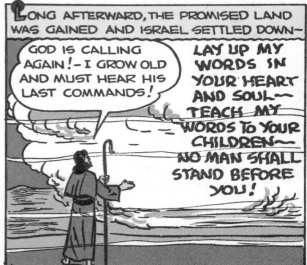

LONG AFTERWARD, THE PROMISED LAND WAS GAINED AND ISRAEL SETTLED DOWN—

GOD IS CALLING AGAIN!—I GROW OLD AND MUST HEAR HIS LAST COMMANDS!

LAY UP MY WORDS IN YOUR HEART AND SOUL~ TEACH MY WORDS TO YOUR CHILDREN~ NO MAN SHALL STAND BEFORE YOU!

AND THE LORD SPOKE UNTO MOSES SAYING:— GO YOU TO THE MOUNTAIN NEBO IN MOAB, BEHOLD THE LAND OF CANAAN WHICH I HAVE GIVEN TO ISRAEL— AND THERE YOU SHALL DIE UPON EARTH— AND MOSES WAS A HUNDRED AND TWENTY YEARS OLD AT HIS DEATH, AND THE PEOPLE WEPT FOR HIM FOR THIRTY DAYS ~~~

THERE WAS NEVER ONE LIKE MOSES BEFORE! HE LED US FROM BONDAGE TO THE PROMISED LAND— WE SHALL ALWAYS REMEMBER HIS NAME!

THE END

THE STORY OF
JOSHUA
PART ONE

ARRANGED FROM THE OLD TESTAMENT BOOK OF JOSHUA--

When Joshua succeeded Moses as leader of the Israelites, he followed God's command to take his people into Canaan, the promised land ---

THE LORD GOD COMMANDED US TO GO FORWARD AND FEAR NOT—IN THREE DAYS, THEREFORE, WE MARCH ACROSS THE RIVER JORDAN!

YES, AFTER FORTY YEARS OF WANDERING, WE NOW REACH CANAAN, THE LAND WHICH GOD PROMISED MOSES!

ALREADY I HAVE SENT SCOUTS AHEAD TO FIND OUT ABOUT THE LAND AND THE PEOPLE ACROSS THE JORDAN—AS SOON AS THEY RETURN, WE SHALL MARCH!

The two scouts go into a house built in the city wall, in which a woman named Rahab lived ~~

PERHAPS RAHAB WILL GIVE US INFORMATION!

LET US GO IN QUICKLY! —WE ARE BEING FOLLOWED!

COME IN, QUICKLY, ERE YOU ARE SEEN! — I SHALL HIDE YOU ON THE ROOF AMONG THE FLAX WHICH IS STACKED THERE TO DRY!

AS RAHAB IS HIDING THEM IN THE FLAX ON THE ROOF, GUARDS COME KNOCKING AT THE DOOR ---

WE KNOW THAT ISRAELITE SCOUTS CAME HERE—TAKE US TO THEM!

YES, THEY CAME HERE BUT THEY HAVE GONE NOW, I KNOW NOT WHERE!

RAHAB GOES BACK TO THE ROOF AND SPEAKS TO THE TWO ISRAELITES ~~~

IF I HELP YOU GET AWAY SAFELY, WILL YOU PROMISE THAT WHEN YOUR ARMIES COME, YOU WILL NOT HARM ME, MY FAMILY OR MY HOUSE!

WE SOLEMNLY PROMISE, RAHAB, TO DO THIS FOR YOU AND YOUR FAMILY —NOW TELL US HOW TO GET AWAY!

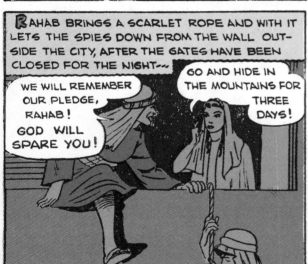

RAHAB BRINGS A SCARLET ROPE AND WITH IT LETS THE SPIES DOWN FROM THE WALL OUTSIDE THE CITY, AFTER THE GATES HAVE BEEN CLOSED FOR THE NIGHT~~~

WE WILL REMEMBER OUR PLEDGE, RAHAB! GOD WILL SPARE YOU!

GO AND HIDE IN THE MOUNTAINS FOR THREE DAYS!

AFTER THREE DAYS THE SCOUTS RETURN SAFELY TO JOSHUA FROM ACROSS THE JORDAN RIVER AND MAKE THEIR REPORT~~~

RAHAB TOLD US THAT THE PEOPLE OF JERICHO ARE TERRIFIED LEST WE CONQUER THEM! THEY FEAR GOD'S ANGER!

GOOD! NOW GIVE THE SIGNAL AND LET OUR ARMIES MARCH TO THE JORDAN!

THE ISRAELITES MARCH

LATER, ALONG THE BANKS OF THE JORDAN RIVER---

FORWARD, ISRAELITES! - LET THE MEN OF GOD GO FIRST! - ACROSS THE JORDAN! - AND THEN - ON TO JERICHO!

AS THE ISRAELITES FOLLOWED JOSHUA AND THE PRIESTS THE WATERS PARTED TO LET THEM WALK ACROSS TO THE OTHER SIDE!

THE ISRAELITES HALTED AT GILGAL AND PITCHED THEIR TENTS FOR A REST---

FOR FORTY YEARS WE HAVE BEEN WANDERING IN THE WILDERNESS WITHOUT A LAND OF OUR OWN—NOW GOD HAS FULFILLED HIS PROMISE! WE ARE IN THE LAND OF CANAAN ON THE EVE OF THE FEAST OF THE PASSOVER!

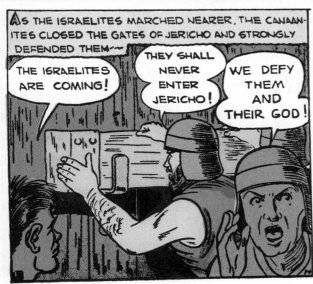

AS THE ISRAELITES MARCHED NEARER, THE CANAAN-ITES CLOSED THE GATES OF JERICHO AND STRONGLY DEFENDED THEM---

THE ISRAELITES ARE COMING!

THEY SHALL NEVER ENTER JERICHO!

WE DEFY THEM AND THEIR GOD!

JOSHUA SPEAKS—

OF OURSELVES WE CAN NEVER BREAK JERICHO'S DEFENSES — BUT GOD HAS SHOWN US A WAY— HEAR ME, PEOPLE OF ISRAEL— ON HOW THE WALLS OF JERICHO WILL FALL! BY GOD'S COMMAND!

GOD REVEALED TO JOSHUA HOW THE ISRAELITES WERE TO OVERCOME THE CITY OF JERICHO—THEY WERE TO WALK AROUND THE WALLS ONCE A DAY FOR SIX DAYS, AND THE PRIESTS WERE TO BLOW THE TRUMPETS—ON THE SEVENTH DAY, THEY WERE ALL TO MARCH AROUND SEVEN TIMES—THE PEOPLE WERE TO SHOUT AND THE WALLS WOULD FALL DOWN—

AND ON THE SEVENTH DAY, THE PRIESTS AND THE PEOPLE MARCHED AROUND THE WALLS SEVEN TIMES—THE PRIESTS BLEW ON THE TRUMPETS—

AND WHEN JOSHUA GAVE THE SIGNAL, THE PEOPLE SHOUTED WITH ALL THEIR MIGHT—

—AND GOD MADE THE WALLS OF JERICHO FALL!

THE ISRAELITES RUSH INTO THE CITY

THIS IS RAHAB'S HOUSE WHICH WE PROMISED TO SPARE IN THE LORD'S NAME!

IT SHALL BE SPARED—BUT THE REST OF THEM HAVE DEFIED GOD!

SO THE CITY OF JERICHO FELL AND THE HEBREWS WENT TO LIVE IN IT — BUT THE REST OF THE LAND OF CANAAN REMAINED UNCONQUERED ~~~

NEXT, WE ATTACK THE CITY OF AI, BUT IT IS STRONG, SO WE MUST PREPARE!

LET US SEND 3,000 MEN AGAINST IT AT ONCE IN A SURPRISE ATTACK!

BUT AT AI, THE ISRAELITES WERE DEFEATED — GOD PUNISHED THEM FOR THE WRONGDOING OF A FEW WHO STOLE BOOTY FROM THE CITY ~~~

THE ISRAELITES SHALL FIND AI WILL NOT BE TAKEN AS WAS JERICHO!

THE LORD HAS DESERTED US — WHY?

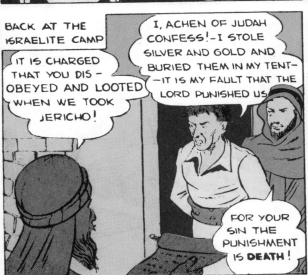

BACK AT THE ISRAELITE CAMP

IT IS CHARGED THAT YOU DIS-OBEYED AND LOOTED WHEN WE TOOK JERICHO!

I, ACHEN OF JUDAH CONFESS! — I STOLE SILVER AND GOLD AND BURIED THEM IN MY TENT — IT IS MY FAULT THAT THE LORD PUNISHED US

FOR YOUR SIN THE PUNISHMENT IS **DEATH**!

AFTER THE WRONGDOER HAD BEEN PUNISHED, THE ISRAELITES RETURNED TO ATTACK AI AGAIN

NOW WE MUST FOOL THE MEN OF AI AND TAKE THE CITY BY A RUSE! — — WE CANNOT CONQUER IT OTHERWISE!

WE SHALL SEND MEN TO ATTACK THE GATES OF AI — SUDDENLY THEY MUST TURN AND RUN AWAY — THE MEN OF AI WILL THINK WE ARE AFRAID AND WILL OPEN THE GATES TO FOLLOW US — BUT WE SHALL HAVE MEN HIDING WHO WILL THEN RUSH INTO THE CITY!

RETREAT NOW, MEN! — NOT TOO FAST, SO THEY WILL OPEN THE GATES AND FOLLOW!

THE ISRAELITES ARE RUNNING OFF! AFTER THEM!

QUICKLY, NOW, WE SHALL CUT OFF THEIR RETREAT AND ENCIRCLE THE MEN OF AI!

WE ARE TRICKED AND SURROUNDED! — WE MUST SURRENDER!

FORWARD, MEN OF ISRAEL! — THROUGH THE GATE! — WE'LL TAKE THE CITY OF AI NOW!

SO BY THIS CLEVER PLAN OF ATTACK, THE ISRAELITES TOOK AI — ITS KING WAS CAPTURED AND HANGED — AND THE ISRAELITES GREW MORE POWERFUL IN CANAAN —

THE KING IS DEAD — AI IS OURS — I WILL GIVE YOU THE LAWS FOR OUR NEW LAND — THEY SHALL BE WRITTEN ON STONE AND PRESERVED!

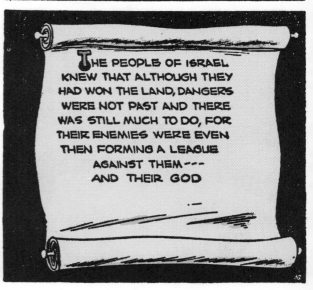

THE PEOPLE OF ISRAEL KNEW THAT ALTHOUGH THEY HAD WON THE LAND, DANGERS WERE NOT PAST AND THERE WAS STILL MUCH TO DO, FOR THEIR ENEMIES WERE EVEN THEN FORMING A LEAGUE AGAINST THEM — AND THEIR GOD

ADONIZEDEK, AMORITE KING OF JERUSALEM, SUMMONS FOUR OTHER AMORITE KINGS TO FORM AN ALLIANCE AND BRING THIER ARMIES TOGETHER---

NONE CAN RESIST US, LEAST OF ALL, THE ISRAELITES !

WE WILL STRIKE FIRST—BUT WE MUST HASTEN !

THE GIBEONITES MAY CAUSE TROUBLE IF WE DELAY !

THE GIBEONITES, FEARING THE STRENGTH OF THE ISRAELITES, SOUGHT TO MAKE A PACT WITH JOSHUA TO PROTECT THEMSELVES, INSTEAD OF UNITING WITH THE OTHER TRIBES TO FIGHT THE ISRAELITES —THEY PRETENDED TO HAVE COME FROM A GREAT DISTANCE, BUT REALLY WERE AN ENEMY TRIBE---

WE ARE POOR AND CANNOT DEFEND OUR—SELVES—YET THE KINGS IN CANAAN HAVE UNITED TO CRUSH US AND YOU !

LATER---

THE GIBEONITES HAVE TRICKED US— THEY ARE A HIVITE PEOPLE AND DO NOT LIVE FAR AWAY !

WE SHALL FIGHT FOR THEM, THOUGH, BECAUSE WE PROMISED TO—BUT WHEN WE WIN, THEY SHALL SERVE US !

THE GIBEONITES, BESIEGED BY THE FIVE KINGS AND THEIR ARMIES, SENT WORD TO JOSHUA TO COME AND HELP THEM—THE FIVE ARMIES ARE BEATEN---

AFTER THEM ! CAPTURE THEIR KINGS!

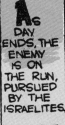 AS DAY ENDS, THE ENEMY IS ON THE RUN, PURSUED BY THE ISRAELITES,

BUT NIGHT GROWS NEAR! THE GROWING DARKNESS WILL SURELY HELP THE FLEEING HORDES ESCAPE!

JOSHUA ASKS FOR A MIRACLE---

SUN, DO NOT SET! MOON, DO NOT RISE! MAY THE LORD DELAY DARKNESS UNTIL OUR ENEMIES ARE DESTROYED--

AND THE SUN DID NOT SET UNTIL THE ENEMY WAS DESTROYED....

LOOK! THE SUN DOES NOT MOVE! EVEN THE HEAVENS FIGHT AGAINST US!

COURAGE, MEN! GOD FIGHTS ON OUR SIDE!

"AND THERE WAS NO DAY LIKE THAT BEFORE IT OR AFTER IT, THAT THE LORD HEARKENED UNTO THE VOICE OF A MAN: FOR THE LORD FOUGHT FOR ISRAEL."

THE STORY OF JOSHUA

PART TWO

FROM THE OLD TESTAMENT BOOKS OF JOSHUA AND JUDGES

JOSHUA'S ARMIES CONTINUED TO GAIN VICTORIES AS CANAAN WAS CONQUERED—HAZOR, A POWERFUL CITY WAS TAKEN AND BURNED TO THE GROUND———

JOSHUA WON BY QUICK MARCHES AND SURPRISE ATTACKS——— EVEN THE TRIBE OF ANAKIM, THE TERROR OF THE ISRAELITES, WERE ROUTED———

FOR SIX YEARS JOSHUA CONTINUED HIS VICTORIES UNTIL THIRTY-ONE KINGS AND THEIR PEOPLE HAD BEEN SUBDUED———

KINGS IN THOSE DAYS WERE TRIBAL CHIEFS, AND OFTEN THEIR CITIES WERE VERY SMALL...

WHEN JOSHUA AND HIS LEADERS HAD CONQUERED NEARLY ALL THE CITIES OF CANAAN, HE STOPPED HIS VICTORIOUS MARCH LONG ENOUGH TO DIVIDE THE LAND AMONG ELEVEN OF THE TWELVE TRIBES OF ISRAEL AS THEIR INHERITANCE — ALL THE PEOPLE NOW KNEW THAT GOD HAD KEPT HIS PROMISE TO MOSES THAT THEY SHOULD HAVE NEW HOMES IN THE PROMISED LAND———

THE ONE TRIBE WHICH WAS GIVEN NO LAND WAS THE LEVITES—

WE HAVE NO LAND, BUT WE ARE THE PRIESTLY TRIBE AND THE OTHER TRIBES GIVE US ONE TENTH OF WHAT THEIR LAND BRINGS FORTH!

THEN SOME ISRAELITES MET TOGETHER TO PLAN HOW THEY MIGHT HONOR JOSHUA, THEIR LEADER---

WE MUST SHOW JOSHUA THAT WE APPRECIATE HIM! —IF IT WEREN'T FOR HIM, WHERE WOULD WE BE?

JUST AS JOSHUA APPORTIONED THE LAND TO US, LET US NOW GIVE HIM LAND FROM OUR INHERITANCE!

A FINE IDEA— LET'S DO IT AT ONCE!

LATER----

JOSHUA, WE WANT YOU TOO, TO HAVE AN INHERITANCE, A REWARD FOR THE GREAT WORK YOU HAVE DONE!

WE SHALL GIVE YOU THE CITY OF TIMNATH-SERAH IN MOUNT EPHRAIM!

THANK YOU! —IN THAT CITY I WILL BUILD A HOUSE— I WILL LIVE THERE AND IT SHALL BE MY HOME!

IT IS LITTLE ENOUGH FOR ALL YOU HAVE DONE!

JOSHUA MADE SIX CITIES--"CITIES OF REFUGE". IF A MAN WHO KILLED ANOTHER BY ACCIDENT, REACHED ONE OF THEM, HE WAS SAFE FROM BLOOD VENGEANCE--

IF I CAN GET THERE, I WILL HAVE A FAIR TRIAL!

CATCH HIM BEFORE HE REACHES THE CITY!

THUS JOSHUA RAISED THE STANDARDS OF JUSTICE...

THEN FOLLOWED A SHORT PERIOD OF PEACE, AS THE ISRAELITES SETTLED DOWN IN THEIR NEW LAND OF CANAAN----

OUR NEW LAND IS NEARLY REBUILT, AFTER OUR TERRIBLE WARS!

YES, AND WE ARE FINDING A MEASURE OF HAPPINESS HERE, FOR JOSHUA IS A WISE RULER.

SO UNDER JOSHUA, ISRAEL WAS GRADUALLY BECOMING A STRONG NATION, AS THEY WON AND WORKED THE LANDS WHICH GOD HAD PROMISED THEM.

THE LORD, YOUR GOD, HAS GIVEN US PEACE, BUT TAKE CARE TO OBEY HIS COMMANDMENTS FOR MOSES TAUGHT US TO LOVE THE LORD AND WALK IN HIS WAYS!

YEARS PASSED AND JOSHUA GREW VERY OLD — ONE DAY HE CALLED THE LEADERS OF ISRAEL TO SPEAK TO THEM~~~

WHY DID YOU CALL US, JOSHUA?

I AM GETTING OLD — WE MUST TALK TOGETHER FOR I HAVE NOT MUCH LONGER TO LIVE!

ALL MY LIFE THE LORD GOD HAS FOUGHT ON OUR SIDE — NOW OUR ENEMIES ARE DESTROYED OR WEAKENED — THOSE WHO REMAIN PAY US ANNUAL TRIBUTE — THE NEW LANDS HAVE BEEN DIVIDED AMONG THE TRIBES OF ISRAEL — BECAUSE OF THESE THINGS, WE MUST BE COURAGEOUS AND EVER LOYAL TO GOD!

CHOOSE THIS DAY WHOM YOU WILL SERVE — THE TRUE GOD OR THE GODS OF THE AMORITES — AS FOR ME, I WILL SERVE THE LORD!

GOD FORBID THAT WE SHOULD FORSAKE THE LORD — WE WILL SERVE THE LORD!

AYE, INDEED WE SHALL SERVE THE LORD GOD!

AT THE AGE OF 110 YEARS JOSHUA DIED — THE PEOPLE OF ISRAEL WERE FILLED WITH SORROW AT HIS BURIAL ~~~

WHEN JOSHUA DIED, LEADERSHIP IN THE WAR AGAINST THE CANAANITES FELL TO THE TRIBES OF SIMEON AND JUDAH ~~~

THE TRIBE OF SIMEON MUST LEAD THE ISRAELITES NOW!

YES, UNITED WE CAN CONQUER, BUT OUR CITIES ARE NOT YET FREE FROM DANGER!

WHEN THE SMALL TRIBE OF SIMEON AND THE POWERFUL TRIBE OF JUDAH UNITED TO FIGHT, THEIR ARMIES FELT CONFIDENT THAT THEY WOULD WIN~~~

LET US FIGHT THE CANAANITES AND PERIZZITES AT ONCE!

AND STOP KING ADONI-BEZEK FROM MAKING THOSE RAIDS AGAINST US!

They struck ferociously at Bezek, the city of King Adoni-Bezek---

There goes the king of the city!

We have slain ten thousand men this day—take the king alive!

The king is captured---

Your city has fallen and so have you!

It is the end for me!

We shall take you to our captain for punishment!

You shall get the punishment a king deserves for doing great wrongs!

Even as I have done, so it is to be done to me!

They took Adoni-Bezek, afterward, to Jerusalem, where he died, unmourned— later, the Israelites went out again, to beat back the Canaan-ites further, to distant mountains and through many valleys ----

So THE TRIBES OF JUDAH AND SIMEON CONQUERED THEIR ENEMIES IN HEBRON AND DEBIR AND IN MANY OTHER PLACES ---

But AS THEY BECAME CONQUERORS, THE CHILDREN OF ISRAEL BEGAN TO FORGET THEIR GOD---

YOU NO LONGER WORSHIP THE LORD GOD! — I MYSELF SAW YOU GO TO THE TEMPLE OF BAAL!

WHAT'S WRONG WITH WORSHIPPING BAAL?

Later MANY ISRAELITES WERE DISLOYAL TO GOD---

BUT WITHOUT GOD'S PROMISED HELP WE WOULD HAVE FAILED! HE IS OUR STRENGTH!

PAH! WE WERE POOR THEN--WE ARE RICH NOW! WHY WORSHIP A GOD WHO DEMANDS SO MUCH OF US?

Suddenly A VOICE IS HEARD!

I AM THE LORD YOUR GOD— YOU HAVE DISOBEYED ME— THEREFORE I WILL NOT DRIVE OUT THE CANAANITES— —THEY WILL BE LEFT HERE TO TEST ISRAEL!

OUR LORD MEANT THAT IF WE DO NOT RETURN TO HIS WAYS, WE SHALL HAVE TROUBLE FOR IF WE ARE NOT FAITHFUL TO HIM, WE SHALL NOT BE ABLE TO CONQUER THE CANAANITES!

The ISRAELITES WERE BEATEN ALSO BY THE MESOPOTAMIAN INVADER, WHO RULED THEM FOR EIGHT YEARS — IN THEIR TROUBLE THEY CRIED TO GOD, WHO SENT THEM A DELIVERER — OTHNIEL, WHO WENT TO WAR AND DROVE OUT THE FOREIGN KING---

YES, WE ARE FREE AGAIN — BUT WHY WERE WE ENSLAVED? BECAUSE WE WERE DISLOYAL TO OUR LORD!

OTHNIEL LED US TO VICTORY --BUT WITH GOD'S HELP! LET US NEVER FORGET THAT!

The Story of DEBORAH

THE WOMAN JUDGE WHO SAVED ISRAEL

FROM THE BOOK OF JUDGES CHAPTERS FOUR AND FIVE

NOT LONG AFTER JOSHUA DIED, ISRAEL AGAIN FORGOT GOD'S WAYS AND TURNED TO RICHES AND PLEASURE ~~

LET'S HAVE FUN INSTEAD OF GOING TO WORSHIP!

KING JABIN INVADE US? THAT'S SILLY TALK!

BUT KING JABIN, OF CANAAN, FOR TWENTY YEARS THE OPPRESSOR OF ISRAEL, DECIDED TO INVADE AGAIN ~~

IT WILL BE EASY TO TAKE ISRAEL!

THEY ARE NOT STRONG ENOUGH TO RESIST!

YOU, GENERAL SISERA, WILL TAKE COMMAND, AND SUBDUE ISRAEL, FOR ME!

THEY DON'T KNOW THE ART OF WAR — I DO! WE'LL WIN AND GRIND THEIR FACES IN THE DIRT, ONCE MORE!

OFF THESE STREETS, YOU!

YOU'LL OBEY SISERA FROM NOW ON!

THE ISRAELITES MOANED ~~

A SAD DAY FOR OUR NATION!

IT IS THE OLD STORY AGAIN--WE HAVE NEGLECTED GOD!

TOO LATE FOR HELP NOW, I FEAR!

OVER ISRAEL RULED A WOMAN JUDGE AND PROPHETESS NAMED DEBORAH--

YES, SOMETHING MUST BE DONE-- I'LL DO IT!

SISERA MAKES SLAVES OF US!

THERE MUST BE SOME WAY OUT!

I'LL HOLD COURT HERE-- CITIES ARE NOT SAFE-- I CAN THINK BETTER!

HERE AT MOUNT EPHRAIM IT'S QUIETER TOO!-- WHAT ARE YOUR PLANS, JUDGE DEBORAH?

GET THOSE ORDERS TO GENERAL BARAK SWIFTLY, MESSENGER!

AT LAST-- WE SHALL FIGHT THIS SISERA!

I WILL GO TO BARAK-- SURELY HE CAN SAVE US!

THE MESSENGER BRINGS BARAK--

I COME, DEBORAH! YOU WISH ME TO CALL UP AN ARMY?

AH, BARAK!-- THE TIME HAS COME-- GOD HAS MADE IT CLEAR THAT YOU MUST GO TO MT. TABOR WITH 10,000 MEN!

OUR CHANCES ARE VERY SLIM, DEBORAH-- I AM UNWILLING TO DO IT UNLESS YOU ALSO GO ALONG!

YOU NEED NOT FEAR-- TOGETHER WE WILL DELIVER ISRAEL!

I FEAR SISERA'S CHARIOTS WILL CUT OUR ARMY TO PIECES!

FAINT HEART! GOD HAS REVEALED THAT SISERA WILL FALL-- AND BY A WOMAN'S HAND!

ARE YOU READY, MEN?

MEN OF ISRAEL, FIGHT FOR GOD AND FREEDOM!

DEBORAH AND BARAK, WE'RE READY!

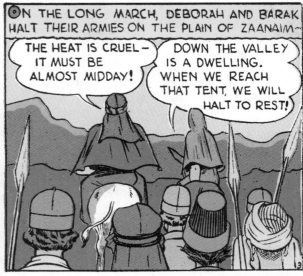

ON THE LONG MARCH, DEBORAH AND BARAK HALT THEIR ARMIES ON THE PLAIN OF ZAANAIM—

THE HEAT IS CRUEL— IT MUST BE ALMOST MIDDAY!

DOWN THE VALLEY IS A DWELLING. WHEN WE REACH THAT TENT, WE WILL HALT TO REST!

THEY REST AT THE TENT OF HEBER, THE KENITE, AS JAEL, HEBER'S WIFE, TALKS LONG WITH DEBORAH, THE WOMAN JUDGE—

I, TOO AM OF KIN TO MOSES— I WISH I WERE A GREAT WOMAN LIKE YOU, TO HELP OUR ARMIES WIN!

EVERYONE CAN DO HIS PART— PERHAPS YOU, TOO, JAEL, WILL HELP US TO VICTORY!

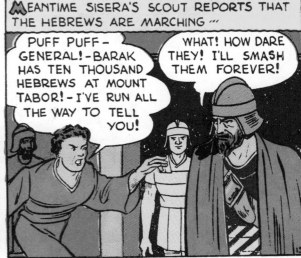

MEANTIME SISERA'S SCOUT REPORTS THAT THE HEBREWS ARE MARCHING—

PUFF PUFF— GENERAL!—BARAK HAS TEN THOUSAND HEBREWS AT MOUNT TABOR!—I'VE RUN ALL THE WAY TO TELL YOU!

WHAT! HOW DARE THEY! I'LL SMASH THEM FOREVER!

MAKE READY MY 900 CHARIOTS! —CRUSH THE HEBREWS UNDER IRON BATTLE-WAGONS!—I'LL TEACH THEM TO DARE TO FIGHT FOR FREEDOM!

MEANWHILE SISERA'S ARMIES MARCHED, SEARCHING FOR THE FORCES OF BARAK—

I MUST MAKE SURE WHERE THEY ARE—CAPTURE THOSE SHEPHERDS—WE'LL MAKE THEM TELL WHERE BARAK MARCHED!

SISERA FLED --- AND BARAK WENT AFTER HIM

NOT A MAN ESCAPED FROM THE HEBREWS BUT SISERA -- BUT HE WAS THE CRUELEST AND MOST DANGEROUS OF THEM ALL ---

JAEL SPEAKS WITH A SERVANT THAT IS THE MIGHTY SISERA!

SISERA!--WHEN HE LEARNS WE ARE KIN OF MOSES HE WILL SURELY KILL US! OH, IF I WERE A MAN, A SOLDIER! THEN I COULD STRIKE A BLOW FOR ISRAEL AND FOR GOD!--BUT I AM ONLY A WOMAN, AND I HAVE NO WEAPONS!

DRINK, THEN LIE DOWN!

I CAN RUN NO MORE-- STAND GUARD OUTSIDE LIKE A SOLDIER, WOMAN, WHILE I SLEEP-- I'LL GET AWAY, RAISE A NEW ARMY AND KILL ALL HEBREW REBELS!

JAEL OUTSIDE THE TENT

HE WILL KILL ME-- OUGHT I KILL HIM? "STAND GUARD LIKE A SOLDIER" THAT'S IT!-- BUT A SOLDIER OF THE LORD GOD!-IF ONLY I HAD A WEAPON!

A SIGN FROM HEAVEN! HERE **ARE** WEAPONS! DEBORAH SAID THAT PERHAPS I, TOO, COULD STRIKE A BLOW TO DELIVER ISRAEL!

HE SLEEPS-- THIS IS THE TIME! I STRIKE FOR ISRAEL!

I HAVE DONE IT! NO LONGER NOW WILL SISERA PERSECUTE THE ISRAELITES! -SO END TWENTY YEARS OF OPPRESSION OF MY PEOPLE! MAY GOD FORGIVE BOTH HIM AND ME!

MEANTIME LOOK--SISERA'S CHARIOT! THIS IS WHERE HE ESCAPED FROM BARAK

THAT'S BAD- SISERA'S A VERY DANGEROUS MAN!

END

THE STORY OF

GIDEON

THE FARMER WARRIOR WHO FREED ISRAEL YET REFUSED TO BECOME HER KING

FROM THE BOOK OF JUDGES, CHAPTERS 6-8

EVERY HARVEST SEASON FOR SEVEN YEARS, THE MIDIANITES AND OTHER TRIBES INVADED ISRAEL, DESTROYING THEIR GRAIN AND TAKING THEIR CATTLE ---

YOU WILL LEARN WHO IS CONQUEROR, AND OBEY!

OW!

THE ISRAELITES ARE FORCED TO FLEE INTO HIDING ---

WE'LL LIVE IN CAVES WHERE WE'LL BE SAFE!

MAY GOD SOON HEAR OUR CRIES FOR DELIVERANCE AND HELP US!

A PROPHET COMES TO THE CHILDREN OF ISRAEL -

I COME TO REMIND YOU OF THE LORD GOD WHO BROUGHT YOU UP FROM EGYPT-FOR YOU HAVE NOT OBEYED HIS VOICE!

YES, THAT IS WHY WE ARE BEING PUNISHED!

AND SO THE JEWS REPENTED ---

YOU SEE, MY CHILDREN, WE MUST ALL TRY TO DO BETTER!

AT ONE PLACE A MAN BESIDE A WINEPRESS SECRETLY THRESHES WHEAT---

HOW LONG I CAN DO THIS, GOD ONLY KNOWS!. IF I'M CAUGHT---

SUDDENLY

GO, GIDEON, AND SAVE ISRAEL FROM THE MIDIANITES!

BUT I AM FROM A POOR FAMILY! NOBODY KNOWS ME - GIVE ME SOME SIGN FROM YOURSELF!

GIDEON OFFERS A KID AND SMALL CAKES AS A SACRIFICE; AND AS HE PLACES THE KID ON A ROCK SUDDENLY---

AN ANGEL STRIKING FIRE!--NOW I KNOW GOD IS WITH ME!

THAT NIGHT GIDEON WITH TEN PICKED MEN SMASHED BAAL, A HEATHEN IDOL ---

DESTROY THIS FALSE GOD AND THE SACRED GROVE!

WE DEFY THE POWER OF BAAL!

GIDEON KNOWS THAT SMASHING THE IDOL MEANS WAR. SO

THIS IS THE CALL TO ARMS!

YES, AND MESSENGERS HAVE BEEN SENT TO OTHER TRIBES WHO WILL MEET HERE!

WE'LL FIGHT!

WE'RE READY, GIDEON!

THOUSANDS COME!

FEARING TO RISK PEOPLE'S LIVES NEEDLESSLY, GIDEON REQUESTS A SIGN FROM THE LORD A FLEECE IS LEFT ON THE GROUND ALL NIGHT, AND NEXT MORNING...

LOOK! THE GRASS IS DRY, BUT THIS FLEECE IS WRINGING WET WITH DEW!

THE FOLLOWING MORNING DEW HAS WET THE GROUND BUT THE FLEECE IS COMPLETELY DRY..

BONE DRY, THOUGH THE GRASS IS SOAKED WITH DEW--NOW SURELY I MUST BELIEVE THAT GOD WILL HELP US!

TO THE HILL OF MOREH WHERE THE ENEMY IS!

WE CAN BEAT THEM-- WE'VE GOT PLENTY OF MEN!

THE LORD SPOKE AGAIN TO GIDEON--

YOU HAVE TOO MANY MEN--SEND SOME HOME AND I WILL REVEAL MY POWER!

YES, LORD! - I OBEY!

MEN, THIS IS WAR! - THOSE WHO WISH, MAY GO HOME!

MANY DO GO HOME, BUT--

THERE ARE YET TOO MANY--SEND THEM ALL DOWN TO THE BROOK TO DRINK!

ONLY A FEW DO NOT KNEEL WHILE DRINKING, THESE REMAIN ON THE ALERT, HOLDING THEIR WEAPONS IN ONE HAND.

ARE THEY THE MEN WHO HAD REFUSED TO KNEEL TO BAAL?

GOD TELLS GIDEON TO PICK OUT THESE 300 MEN

NOW RUN AND PICK OUT ONLY THOSE WHO HAVE REFUSED TO KNEEL TO DRINK!! - SEND THE REST HOME!

BUT GIDEON, WE'LL HAVE ONLY THREE HUNDRED MEN!

MEN, GOD HAS PICKED YOU FOR A TOUGH ASSIGNMENT, BUT YOU WILL WIN!

THE MIDIANITES APPROACH AND PITCH THEIR TENTS IN THE VALLEY BELOW…

THEY'VE PITCHED CAMP! NOW WE WILL WORK OUT A PLAN OF ATTACK!

GIDEON KNOWS HE MUST USE STRATEGY WITH SO FEW MEN--HE CREEPS TO THE OUTSIDE OF THE MIDIANITE TENTS AT NIGHT AND OVERHEARS…

I HAD A STRANGE DREAM- A CAKE OF BARLEY BREAD CAME TUMBLING IN UPON US AND DESTROYED OUR CAMP!

THIS MEANS THAT GOD WILL DELIVER US MIDIANITES INTO GIDEON'S HANDS!

GIDEON NOW CALLS HIS MEN TOGETHER AFTER MIDNIGHT, AND EXPLAINS HIS PLANS

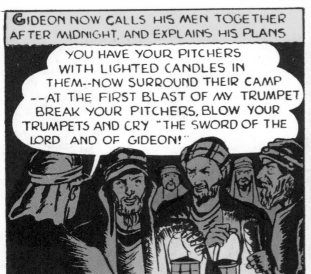

YOU HAVE YOUR PITCHERS WITH LIGHTED CANDLES IN THEM--NOW SURROUND THEIR CAMP --AT THE FIRST BLAST OF MY TRUMPET BREAK YOUR PITCHERS, BLOW YOUR TRUMPETS AND CRY "THE SWORD OF THE LORD AND OF GIDEON!"

WHEN GIDEON BLEW HIS TRUMPET HIS MEN DID AS INSTRUCTED-

THE SWORD OF THE LORD AND OF GIDEON!
THE SWORD OF THE LORD AND OF GIDEON!

AN OVERPOWERING ARMY! WE ARE SURROUNDED!!

THE SUDDEN NIGHT ATTACK AND THE SHOUTING BRING TERROR TO THE CAMP OF THE MIDIANITES- AND THEY FLEE IN PANIC ~

THE PLAN WORKED-- THE MIDIANITES TAKE EACH OTHER FOR AN ENEMY! AFTER THEM! LET NOT A MAN ESCAPE!

OTHER TRIBES OF ISRAEL, NOW AROUSED, ALSO PURSUED THE FLEEING OPPRESSORS.

LOOK, THE EPHRAIMITES ARE JOINING US!

YES, AND THEY'VE CAPTURED THE TWO PRINCES, OREB AND ZEEB!

AFTER THE BATTLE IS WON

ALTHOUGH ENTREATED TO SERVE AS KING, GIDEON REFUSES ...

ISRAEL HAD FORTY YEARS OF PEACE!

AND THOUGH GIDEON REFUSED TO BECOME KING OF ISRAEL HE LIVED LONG AND HAD MANY SONS ...

END

THE STORY OF SAMSON

CHAPTERS 13 THROUGH 16.
FROM THE BOOK OF JUDGES.

SAMSON LIVED IN THE DAYS WHEN THE PHILISTINES WERE CONQUERORS OF PALESTINE. HIS PARENTS HOPED THAT ONE DAY THIS BABY WOULD GROW UP TO FREE THE HEBREWS FROM THEIR OPRESSORS~~

THE HAIR OF HIS HEAD SHALL NEVER BE CUT, A SIGN WE HAVE DEDICATED HIM TO GOD!

SAMSON, NOW A YOUNG MAN, DECIDED TO GO ABOUT AMONG THE PHILISTINES, TO KNOW THEM BETTER, SO HE COULD DEFEAT THEM ~~

I'LL GO AMONG THE PHILISTINES - BUT LOOK! - A YOUNG LION!

SAMSON IS STRONG ENOUGH TO KILL THE LION WITH HIS BARE HANDS ~~

GOD HAS GIVEN ME THIS GREAT STRENGTH!

SAMSON MET A WOMAN OF THE PHILISTINES WHOM HE ASKED IN MARRIAGE —

I WILL MAKE YOU MY WIFE!

SAMPSON FINDS THE DEAD BODY OF THE LION WITH BEES MAKING HONEY, OF WHICH HE EATS, TAKING SOME HOME

AT THE WEDDING FEAST SAMSON PROPOSES A RIDDLE TO THE SNEERING PHILISTINES ~~

IF YOU CAN ANSWER THIS RIDDLE WITHIN SEVEN DAYS, I WILL GIVE YOU THIRTY COATS AND SHIRTS — IF YOU FAIL, YOU MUST GIVE ME A LIKE NUMBER:-"OUT OF THE EATER CAME FOOD!-OUT OF THE STRONG CAME FORTH SWEETNESS!"

ON THE SEVENTH DAY, STILL UNABLE TO ANSWER THE RIDDLE, THEY WENT TO SAMSON'S WIFE ~~~~

ENTICE YOUR HUSBAND TO GET THE ANSWER—WE ARE ANGRY!

YOU GET THE ANSWER FROM HIM—DO YOU HEAR!

IF YOU DON'T WE'LL BURN YOUR HOUSE!

SAMSON'S WIFE KEPT CRYING AND NAGGING HIM TO TELL HER THE RIDDLE ~~~~

YOU DON'T LOVE ME, SAMSON, FOR YOU GIVE MY PEOPLE A RIDDLE AND DON'T TELL ME THE ANSWER!

ALL RIGHT— I SHALL TELL YOU THE ANSWER!

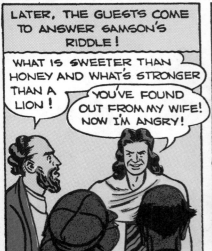

LATER, THE GUESTS COME TO ANSWER SAMSON'S RIDDLE!

WHAT IS SWEETER THAN HONEY AND WHAT'S STRONGER THAN A LION!

YOU'VE FOUND OUT FROM MY WIFE! NOW I'M ANGRY!

SAMSON PAYS HIS WAGER BY TAKING GOODS AWAY FROM 30 PHILISTINES WHOM HE KILLS— HE RETURNS TO HIS FATHER'S HOUSE ~~

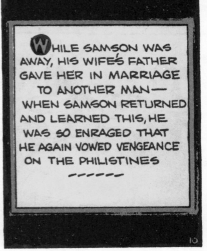

WHILE SAMSON WAS AWAY, HIS WIFE'S FATHER GAVE HER IN MARRIAGE TO ANOTHER MAN— WHEN SAMSON RETURNED AND LEARNED THIS, HE WAS SO ENRAGED THAT HE AGAIN VOWED VENGEANCE ON THE PHILISTINES ~~~~

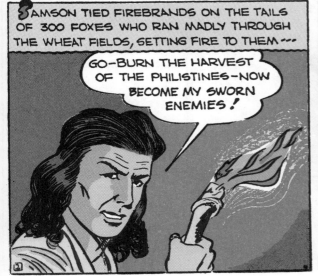

SAMSON TIED FIREBRANDS ON THE TAILS OF 300 FOXES WHO RAN MADLY THROUGH THE WHEAT FIELDS, SETTING FIRE TO THEM ~~~

GO—BURN THE HARVEST OF THE PHILISTINES—NOW BECOME MY SWORN ENEMIES!

THE PHILISTINES WERE ENRAGED AT WHAT SAMSON HAD DONE ~~~~

WE WILL BURN THE WOMAN AND HER FATHER WITH FIRE BECAUSE THEY ANGERED SAMSON—WE WILL ALSO PAY SAMSON FOR WHAT HE'S DONE!

WHILE THE PHILISTINES HUNTED SAMSON WITH AN ARMY, HIS OWN COUNTRYMEN, FEARING THE VENGEANCE OF THEIR CONQUERORS, DELIVERED HIM TO THEM—

DON'T KILL ME!

WE'LL BIND YOU BUT NOT KILL YOU!

THE PHILISTINES ARE OUR RULERS —YOU WILL GET US IN TROUBLE WITH THEM!

WE'LL LEAD YOU INTO THE PHILISTINES' CAMP BOUND!

HIS COUNTRYMEN ARE BRINGING SAMSON TO US—WE'LL PUNISH HIM NOW!

HE BURNED THE WHEAT!

GOD—GIVE ME STRENGTH TO FIGHT THEM!

SAMSON RECEIVED STRENGTH OF THE LORD AND IN A BURST OF ENERGY SNAPPED HIS BONDS AND SNATCHED UP A BONE FROM THE GROUND

WITH THE JAWBONE OF AN ASS I WILL FIGHT MY ENEMIES!

I WILL SLAY THESE MEN!

WITH HIS SUPERNATURAL STRENGTH SAMSON KILLED 1000 OF HIS ENEMIES!

I HAVE DESTROYED THE PHILISTINE ARMY! NOW I SHALL RULE MY OWN PEOPLE!

AND DURING THE NEXT TWENTY YEARS SAMSON RULED AS A JUDGE OVER ISRAEL!

Samson comes to love a girl named Delilah— secretly she had agreed to spy for the Philistines ~~~

THE PHILISTINES HAVE ASKED ME TO FIND OUT WHERE HIS STRENGTH LIES!

WHAT WORRIES YOU, DELILAH? YOU SHOULD BE HAPPY!

The Philistines promised Delilah hundreds of pieces of silver if she could learn the secret of Samson's strength~~

TELL ME, I PRAY, WHEREIN DOES YOUR GREAT STRENGTH LIE?

Samson suspects a trick and does not reveal his secret ~~~~

BIND ME WITH SEVEN GREEN STRANDS AND I SHALL BE WEAK!

Later, the Philistines gave her the seven strands, and she found Samson willing to be bound~~~

I SHALL SEE IF YOU CAN BREAK THESE BONDS!

WE SHALL SEE!

AND WHO ARE THOSE MEN HIDING THERE?

IT IS THE PHILISTINES, SAMSON!

HO! THEY FLEE! —THEY HAD BETTER, OR I'LL BREAK THEM ALL!

SO FAR YOU HAVE NOT ANSWERED MY QUESTION— YOU HAVE TOLD ME ONLY LIES!

BUT STILL SAMSON DID NOT TRUST DELILAH~~

IF YOU WILL BIND ME WITH NEW ROPES, I SHALL HAVE NO MORE POWER!

GETTING THE NEW ROPE, DELILAH AGAIN BINDS SAMSON!

LET'S SEE IF YOU HAVE TOLD ME THE TRUTH!

IT IS ALL IN FUN, DELILAH!

THE NEW ROPES SNAP UNDER SAMSON'S POWER~~

AGAIN YOU MOCK ME, SAMSON! — WHY WILL YOU NOT TELL ME, IF YOU CARE FOR ME AT ALL?

DELILAH GAVE SAMSON NO REST, AND FINALLY ONE DAY——

ALL RIGHT, I'LL TELL YOU — MY HAIR HAS NEVER BEEN CUT, AS A PLEDGE TO GOD — IF IT WERE CUT, MY STRENGTH WOULD GO!

DELILAH COAXED SAMSON TO GO TO SLEEP AND LET THE PHILISTINES IN TO CUT OFF HIS HAIR~~

SEE, HE HAS NO FIGHT IN HIM!

YOU HAVE CUT OFF MY HAIR—MY STRENGTH IS GONE NOW!

THEY HAVE JAILED ME, BLINDED ME AND CHAINED ME — I AM SURELY BEING PUNISHED FOR BREAKING MY VOW TO GOD!

SAMSON FEELS HIS STRENGTH RETURNING ---

MY HAIR IS GROWING FAST— WHEN MY POWER RETURNS I'LL HAVE MY VENGEANCE, BLIND THOUGH I AM!

THE PHILISTINES WENT TO THE TEMPLE NEXT THE JAIL TO WORSHIP THEIR HEATHEN GOD "DAGON" ---

WE SHALL CELEBRATE BENEATH THE NOSE OF THIS SAMSON!

HIS GOD IS HELPLESS— AS HE IS NOW!

NOW BRING IN SAMSON, SO WE MAY MAKE SPORT OF HIM!

YES, WE WANT HIM!

WE'LL GET HIM!

SAMSON, BROUGHT IN BY A SMALL BOY, WAS PUT BETWEEN TWO GREAT PILLARS ---

LAD, PLACE MY HANDS, ONE ON EACH PILLAR—I CANNOT SEE, YOU KNOW!

YES, SIR!

LORD, I CALL ON YOU FOR STRENGTH ONCE MORE! ONLY THIS ONCE, THAT I MAY AVENGE THE LOSS OF MY EYES!

SEE! SAMSON'S STRENGTH HAS RETURNED!

LET ME DIE WITH THEM LORD!- MY LAST ACT!

WE'LL BE KILLED!

SO THE TEMPLE FELL ON THE EVIL PHILISTINES AND SAMSON PERISHED TOO --- HE SLEW THEREFORE AT HIS DEATH MORE THAN HE SLEW DURING HIS LIFE ---

END

The Story of RUTH

NAOMI, A HEBREW WIDOW HAD TWO SONS WHO DIED IN THE LAND OF MOAB. WHILE RETURNING TO HER HOME IN JUDAH, SHE TRIED TO PERSUADE HER TWO DAUGHTERS-IN-LAW TO STAY WITH THEIR OWN PEOPLE IN MOAB.

ARRANGED FROM THE OLD TESTAMENT BOOK OF RUTH

ONE OF THEM RETURNED, BUT THE OTHER, RUTH, INSISTED ON GOING WITH NAOMI TO JUDAH--

"FOR WHITHER THOU GOEST, I WILL GO, AND WHERE THOU LODGEST, I WILL LODGE. THY PEOPLE SHALL BE MY PEOPLE, AND THY GOD MY GOD."

IT WAS THE BEGINNING OF THE BARLEY HARVEST AND THEY PAUSED AT THE FIELDS OF A WEALTHY MAN ----

IT IS BOAZ, KINSMAN OF MY HUSBAND, AND A MAN OF WEALTH!

LET US GLEAN EARS OF CORN IN HIS FIELD AND FIND GRACE IN HIS SIGHT!

HERE I SHALL STAY, AND YOU SHALL ABIDE ALSO! AND GO AND GLEAN IN THE FIELDS OF BOAZ IF IT IS YOUR WISH, RUTH!

I SHALL GO THIS DAY!

SO RUTH ENTERED THE FIELDS OF BOAZ AND TOOK PART IN THE GLEANING OF THE BARLEY-

I SHALL ASK MY SERVANTS WHO THIS GIRL IS!

TELL ME OF THIS GIRL!

IT IS RUTH, NAOMI'S DAUGHTER-IN-LAW, SIRE — NAOMI WHOSE HUSBAND WAS A KINSMAN OF YOURS!

RUTH IT IS, WHO GLEANED, AND WOULD FOLLOW HER MOTHER-IN-LAW, NAOMI, WHEREVER SHE WENT—— SHE IS A MOABITESS, AND IS NOW IN A STRANGE LAND!!

YOU NEED NOT WORK HERE, RUTH! —BUT STAY AND LIVE AMONG US ANYWAY, AND YOU SHALL FIND YOUR NEW HOME HAPPY, AMONG MY PEOPLE!

YOU ARE KIND TO ME, A STRANGER, IN A STRANGE LAND!

I KNOW THAT YOU LEFT YOUR LAND TO FOLLOW NAOMI, AND THE LORD WILL BLESS YOU!

BOAZ GOES AMONG THE REAPERS AND SPEAKS TO THEM OF RUTH ~~

DO NOT REPROACH THIS GIRL, RUTH— INSTEAD LET HER GLEAN AMONG THE SHEAVES AND LET HANDFULS FALL ON PURPOSE FOR HER TO GLEAN!

RUTH GLEANS UNTIL EVENING, AND BEATING OUT HER GLEANING, PREPARES TO TAKE IT TO NAOMI ~~

NAOMI WILL NEED THIS, AND WELCOME IT, AND I SHALL HAVE REPAID HER A LITTLE FOR HER GOODNESS TOWARD ME!

I WORKED IN THE FIELDS OF BOAZ TODAY, AND BROUGHT BARLEY HOME TO YOU, NAOMI

TELL ME ALL ABOUT IT, MY DEAR!

So RUTH WORKED TO THE END OF THE BARLEY HARVEST AND STAYED ON TO WORK THE WHEAT HARVEST---

I AM PLEASED WITH YOUR WORK, RUTH!

ONE DAY, NAOMI SPOKE CONFIDENTIALLY TO RUTH, HER DAUGHTER-IN-LAW---

TONIGHT, BOAZ WINNOWS IN THE THRESHING FLOOR—DRESS WELL, AND GO QUIETLY THERE AND WATCH—WHEN HE HAS FINISHED AND HAS EATEN, GO UP TO HIM!

I OBEY, NAOMI!

LATER---

I HAVE FINISHED WINNOWING—NOW FOR FOOD AND THEN A REST

WHEN HE HAS FINISHED, I SHALL GO TO HIM, BUT NOT BEFORE!

I SHALL REST HERE, FOR THERE IS MUCH TO DO ON THE MORROW, AND I MUST BE UP EARLY!

NOW IT IS TIME!

I AM RUTH, YOUR HANDMAIDEN, WHOM YOU LET WORK IN THE FIELDS!

WH-?

EVERY DAY RUTH WORKED IN THE FIELDS OF BOAZ, WHOM SHE NOW LOVED; AND EACH DAY BOAZ WATCHED HER AND WAS PLEASED~~

THIS RUTH, THE MOABITESS, IS FAVORED OF OUR MASTER! AND SHE WORKS WELL INDEED!

ONE DAY, BOAZ WAS SITTING IDLY BY, WHEN A KINSMAN OF HIS APPEARED~~~

TURN ASIDE AND SIT HERE A MOMENT, KINSMAN!

NOW I SHALL SEEK TEN MEN OF THE ELDERS OF THE CITY AS WITNESSES - DO WAIT FOR ME, HERE, FOR IT'S IMPORTANT!

A LITTLE WHILE LATER ~~~

ACCORDING TO THE LAW, AND SO THAT I HAVE WITNESSES, I WILL BUY THE LAND OF NAOMI, AND GIVE YOU TESTIMONY- FOR THIS I HAVE CALLED YOU!

YOU ARE ALL WITNESSES THIS DAY THAT I MAKE KNOWN THE WISH TO BUY NAOMI'S LAND- AND ALL THE PROPERTY OF ELIMELECH, HER HUSBAND! -AND THAT I WILL PURCHASE FROM YOU THE RIGHT TO TAKE RUTH, THE MOABITESS, AS MY WIFE!

5

BUT, ACCORDING TO LAW I CANNOT OBTAIN THIS LAND- ONLY MY KINSMAN, HERE, MAY DO SO BEFORE ME!

YOU MAY REDEEM _MY_ RIGHT TO BUY THE LAND, BOAZ, AND AS A SIGN ACCORDING TO LAW, I SHALL GIVE YOU MY SHOE IN TESTIMONY!

YOU WITNESS, THEN, THAT I HAVE PURCHASED THE RIGHT TO BUY THIS LAND—AND THE RIGHT TO TAKE RUTH, THE MOABITESS, AS MY WIFE?

WE DO!

YES!

MAY THE LORD, MAKE THIS WOMAN THAT IS COME TO YOUR HOME, LIKE OUR GOOD WOMEN WHO BUILDED THE LANDS OF ISRAEL! BE YOU WORTHY AND GROW FAMOUS IN BETHLEHEM!

SO IT CAME ABOUT THAT BOAZ BOUGHT NAOMI'S LANDS, AND ASKED RUTH TO BE HIS WIFE—

I AM HAPPY, BOAZ, THAT I FIND FAVOR WITH YOU!

YES!

SHE CAME TO US IN FAITH AND WILL MAKE A BRAVE WIFE FOR YOU, BOAZ!

BOAZ TOOK RUTH TO HIS HOUSE—

YOU SHALL HENCEFORTH BE MY WIFE, AND WE SHALL LOVE ONE ANOTHER, RUTH!

NAOMI WAS HAPPY AND PROVIDED FOR, IN HER OLD AGE—

RUTH SHALL MAKE MY HUSBAND'S KINSMAN, BOAZ, VERY HAPPY! SHE WILL CLING TO HIM AS SHE FOLLOWED ME IN LOVE AND KINDNESS!

IN TIME, A SON WAS BORN TO BOAZ ~

YOUR SON, BOAZ

YES, RUTH!

AT NAOMI'S HOUSE ~~~

BLESSED ARE YOU AND YOUR HOUSE, NAOMI, FOR RUTH HAS GIVEN BIRTH TO A BOY THIS DAY!

WE SHALL NAME HIM OBED, MY DEAR, AND HE SHALL BE FAMOUS IN HIS TIME!

AND THEY CALLED HIS NAME OBED, WHO BECAME THE FATHER OF JESSE, WHO IN TURN WAS FATHER OF THE GREAT DAVID YET TO BE BORN!

THUS BEGAN A FAMOUS LINE OF ISRAEL, AND THEY WERE HAPPY ALL THE DAYS OF THEIR LIVES!

THE END

The Story of SAMUEL

FROM THE BOOKS OF FIRST AND SECOND SAMUEL

ON MOUNT EPHRAIM IN THE ANCIENT KINGDOM OF ISRAEL, THERE LIVED A MAN NAMED ELKANAH, WITH HIS WIFE HANNAH--ONCE EACH YEAR THEY WENT UP TO THE CITY OF SHILOH~

HANNAH, WHY ARE YOU CRYING? DON'T YOU KNOW I LOVE YOU? AREN'T WE GOING TOGETHER TO SHILOH TO WORSHIP IN THE GREAT TEMPLE?

I KNOW ELKANAH BUT I AM UNHAPPY BECAUSE WE HAVE NO SON!

IN THE TEMPLE OF THE LORD WHERE ELI WAS HIGH PRIEST, HANNAH PRAYED THAT SHE MIGHT HAVE A SON~

O LORD OF HOSTS, IF YOU WILL BLESS ME WITH A MAN-CHILD, I WILL GIVE HIM TO SERVE YOU ALL THE DAYS OF HIS LIFE!

THIS WOMAN ACTS STRANGELY, FATHER!

PERHAPS SHE HAS TAKEN TOO MUCH WINE AT THE FEAST!

HER LIPS MOVE, BUT HER VOICE IS NOT HEARD!

NO, ELI, I HAVE DRUNK NO WINE - IN GRIEF HAVE I POURED OUT MY SOUL BEFORE THE LORD!

I AND MY SONS, THE PRIESTS HOPHNI AND PHINEHAS, WERE WATCHING YOU-GO IN PEACE AND GOD WILL ANSWER YOUR PRAYER!

AFTER THEY HAD RETURNED TO THEIR HOME IN RAMAH, ELI'S WORDS CAME TRUE- HANNAH GAVE BIRTH TO A BABY SON~

I WILL NAME YOU SAMUEL BECAUSE THAT MEANS "ASKED OF GOD!"

THREE YEARS LATER ~~~

AND AS I VOWED, ELI, I BRING MY SON SAMUEL TO YOU-I AM LENDING HIM TO GOD!

HE WILL LIVE HERE WITH ME IN THE TEMPLE - AND LEARN TO SERVE GOD!

I'LL BE A GOOD BOY MOTHER!

1

So Samuel lived at the temple, helping old Eli and the priests, his sons ~

NOW THE LAMP WILL BURN BRIGHTLY ELI!

YOU ARE A GOOD CHILD—I WISH MY OWN SONS WERE AS GOOD!

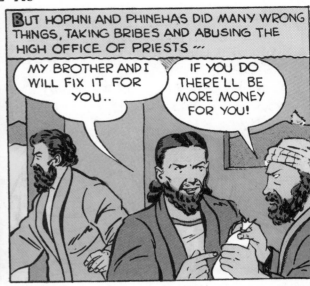

But Hophni and Phinehas did many wrong things, taking bribes and abusing the high office of priests ~

MY BROTHER AND I WILL FIX IT FOR YOU..

IF YOU DO THERE'LL BE MORE MONEY FOR YOU!

One night, Samuel thinks he hears a voice calling ~

SAMUEL!

IT MUST BE ELI CALLING —I'M COMING ELI!

HERE I AM!—I HEARD YOU CALLING!

I DIDN'T CALL YOU, SAMUEL! GO AND LIE DOWN!

—After this had happened three times—

IF THE VOICE CALLS AGAIN, YOU MUST ANSWER "SPEAK, LORD!" FOR IT IS THE LORD GOD CALLING YOU!

I WILL, ELI!

Later—

SAMUEL!

SPEAK, LORD! FOR I LISTEN!

I WILL JUDGE ELI, BECAUSE HIS SONS HAVE MADE THEM-SELVES VILE, AND HE HAS NOT STOPPED THEM! - I WILL MAKE AN END OF ELI AND HIS FAMILY!

LATER SAMUEL TELLS ELI WHAT THE LORD TOLD HIM~

DON'T HIDE FROM ME ANYTHING THAT GOD SAID TO YOU!

HE SAID THAT HE WOULD DESTROY YOU, PHINEHAS AND HOPHNI!

AND THEN WAR CAME BETWEEN SAMUEL'S PEOPLE ISRAEL, AND THE LAND OF THE PHILISTINES—ISRAEL LOST A GREAT BATTLE-TO HEARTEN THE DIS-COURAGED ARMY, ELI'S SONS, THE PRIESTS HOPHNI AND PHINEHAS, CARRIED INTO THE ISRAELITE CAMP, THE ARK OF THE COV-ENANT FROM THE GREAT TEMPLE – A HOLY CHEST IN WHICH WERE KEPT THE TABLETS OF THE LAW AND OTHER SACRED OBJECTS ~

- BUT IN THE BACKGROUND THE EVIL PHILISTINES WERE WATCHING ~

WE MUST FIGHT HARDER THAN EVER!

WHO SHALL DELIVER US OUT OF THE HANDS OF THEIR GOD?

WE MUST CAPTURE THE ARK!

THE PHILISTINES ATTACK ~

THE HOLY ARK MAKES THEM STRONG! - WE'LL KILL THEIR PRIESTS AND CAPTURE IT!

FORWARD! SEIZE THE ARK!

WE ARE LOST, HOPHNI!

THE SONS OF ELI WERE SLAIN AND THE HOLY ARK WAS CAPTURED ~

WHEN NEWS OF THE DEFEAT WAS BROUGHT TO OLD ELI...

WHAT DID YOU SAY TO HIM?

THAT HOPHNI AND PHINEHAS ARE SLAIN AND THAT THE ARK IS TAKEN BY THE PHILISTINES - AND HE FELL AND DIED!

THE PHILISTINES CARRIED THE HOLY ARK TO THE CITY OF ASHDOD, WHERE THEY PUT IT IN THE TEMPLE OF THEIR GOD, DAGON - AND THEN STRANGE THINGS HAPPENED...

THE IMAGE OF DAGON IS SMASHED!

THE POWER OF THE HEBREW GOD HAS DONE THIS!

AND THE PEOPLE WERE AFFLICTED WITH ILLNESS...

NEVER WERE TIMES SO BAD! SO MANY PEOPLE SICK!

THIS PLAGUE HITS RICH AND POOR ALIKE!

THIS NEVER HAPPENED TILL WE CAPTURED THE ARK - I SAY, GIVE IT BACK!

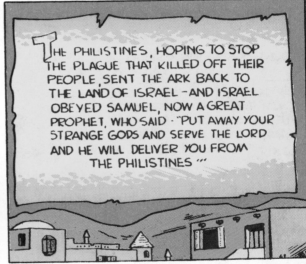

THE PHILISTINES, HOPING TO STOP THE PLAGUE THAT KILLED OFF THEIR PEOPLE, SENT THE ARK BACK TO THE LAND OF ISRAEL - AND ISRAEL OBEYED SAMUEL, NOW A GREAT PROPHET, WHO SAID · "PUT AWAY YOUR STRANGE GODS AND SERVE THE LORD AND HE WILL DELIVER YOU FROM THE PHILISTINES "...

YEARS PASSED...

THE PHILISTINES ARE BEATEN, AND I HAVE TRIED TO SERVE JUSTLY AS A PROPHET AND JUDGE!

SAMUEL IS GOOD, BUT HIS SONS ARE BAD LIKE ELI'S WERE!

WE'RE TIRED OF BEING RULED BY PEOPLE LIKE THAT!

WE SHOULD HAVE A KING!

YOU ARE GOOD, SAMUEL, BUT YOUR SONS ARE NOT LIKE YOU!

HOLY MEN HAVE ALWAYS RULED US IN ISRAEL NOW WE WANT A KING

GIVE US A KING, SAMUEL, LIKE OTHER NATIONS HAVE!

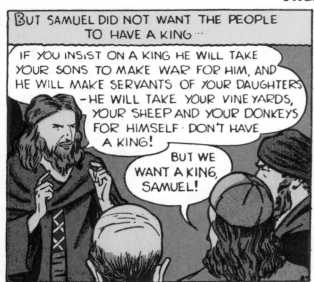

BUT SAMUEL DID NOT WANT THE PEOPLE TO HAVE A KING...

IF YOU INSIST ON A KING HE WILL TAKE YOUR SONS TO MAKE WAR FOR HIM, AND HE WILL MAKE SERVANTS OF YOUR DAUGHTERS - HE WILL TAKE YOUR VINEYARDS, YOUR SHEEP AND YOUR DONKEYS FOR HIMSELF · DON'T HAVE A KING!

BUT WE WANT A KING, SAMUEL!

SO SAMUEL TALKED TO GOD OF ALL THAT HAD HAPPENED ~

LISTEN TO THE VOICE OF THE PEOPLE, SAMUEL, AND GIVE THEM A KING ~ I WILL LEAD YOU TO CHOOSE A GOOD MAN!

THAT WAS THE TIME WHEN THE YOUNG MAN SAUL CAME TO SAMUEL - SAUL WHO WAS THE SON OF KISH AND WHO CAME INTO SAMUEL'S COUNTRY, SEEKING TO FIND HIS FATHER'S DONKEYS WHICH HAD STRAYED AWAY...

EVEN NOW I KNOW THAT THE FUTURE KING OF ISRAEL IS COMING NEAR!

WE'VE COME SO FAR AND NO SIGN OF THE DONKEYS! - BUT THE GREAT PROPHET SAMUEL LIVES HERE - LET'S ASK HIM TO HELP US, SAUL!

YES!

MY NAME IS SAUL - CAN YOU TELL ME WHERE TO FIND THE PROPHET SAMUEL?

I AM HE! YOU ARE EXPECTED - GO UP TO MY HOUSE AND YOU SHALL STAY WITH ME!

THE NEXT MORNING, AFTER A GREAT FEAST...

DON'T WORRY ABOUT THE LOST DONKEYS - THEY HAVE BEEN FOUND, SAUL - BUT GREATER NEWS THAN THAT - YOU ARE TO BE A PROPHET AND THE FIRST KING OF ISRAEL!

BUT I COME FROM A POOR AND HUMBLE FAMILY! - WHY THIS HONOR?

SAMUEL SUMMONED ALL THE PEOPLE OF ISRAEL TO BEHOLD THEIR NEW KING, SAUL ...

THIS IS HE WHOM THE LORD HAS CHOSEN TO BE YOUR KING - AND THERE IS NONE LIKE HIM!

GOD SAVE THE KING!

GOD SAVE KING SAUL!

AS KING, SAUL FOUGHT MANY BATTLES AGAINST THE PHILISTINE AND TRIUMPHED!

WITH SAUL AS KING, WE ALWAYS WIN NOW!

A GREAT FIGHTER!

ONCE, BEFORE A BATTLE, SAMUEL PROMISED TO COME AND OFFER UP A SACRIFICE SO THE ISRAELITE ARMIES WOULD WIN—BUT SAMUEL WAS LATE ~

WHY DOESN'T SAMUEL COME AS PROMISED?—THE PHILIS-TINES MAY ATTACK ANY MOMENT—I'LL OFFER THE SACRIFICE MYSELF!

BUT YOU WERE LATE, AND I THOUGHT I WOULD DO IT MYSELF!

IMPATIENT KING, YOU HAVE OFFENDED GOD!—YOU DID WRONG!

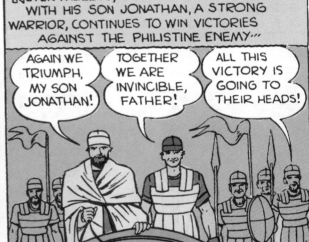

NEVERTHELESS, SAUL REMAINS KING AND WITH HIS SON JONATHAN, A STRONG WARRIOR, CONTINUES TO WIN VICTORIES AGAINST THE PHILISTINE ENEMY ~

AGAIN WE TRIUMPH, MY SON JONATHAN!

TOGETHER WE ARE INVINCIBLE, FATHER!

ALL THIS VICTORY IS GOING TO THEIR HEADS!

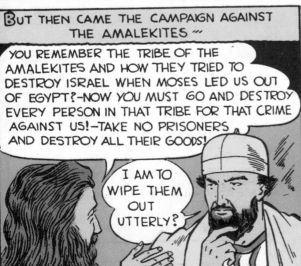

BUT THEN CAME THE CAMPAIGN AGAINST THE AMALEKITES ~

YOU REMEMBER THE TRIBE OF THE AMALEKITES AND HOW THEY TRIED TO DESTROY ISRAEL WHEN MOSES LED US OUT OF EGYPT?—NOW YOU MUST GO AND DESTROY EVERY PERSON IN THAT TRIBE FOR THAT CRIME AGAINST US!—TAKE NO PRISONERS AND DESTROY ALL THEIR GOODS!

I AM TO WIPE THEM OUT UTTERLY?

AGAIN SAUL'S ARMIES WERE VICTORIOUS, BUT HE DISOBEYED SAMUEL—HE SPARED THE KING OF THE AMALEKITES, AND OUT OF GREED, CAPTURED MANY FAT SHEEP, OXEN AND LAMBS ~

SAMUEL, ANGRY, REBUKES SAUL FOR HIS DISOBEDIENCE ~

I DID DISOBEY, BUT IT WASN'T MY FAULT!

YOU HAVE REJECTED THE WORD OF GOD AND DISOBEYED HIM - TO OBEY IS BETTER THAN SACRIFICE - GOD HAS REJECTED YOU AS KING OF ISRAEL!

AND FROM THAT DAY SAMUEL NEVER LOOKED ON SAUL'S FACE AGAIN ~

IF ONLY SAUL HADN'T FAILED AS KING!

HOW LONG WILL YOU MOURN FOR HIM? NOW YOU MUST FIND A NEW KING FOR ISRAEL - GO TO BETHLEHEM AND I WILL SHOW YOU WHAT TO DO!

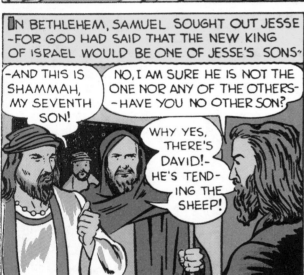

IN BETHLEHEM, SAMUEL SOUGHT OUT JESSE - FOR GOD HAD SAID THAT THE NEW KING OF ISRAEL WOULD BE ONE OF JESSE'S SONS ~

- AND THIS IS SHAMMAH, MY SEVENTH SON!

NO, I AM SURE HE IS NOT THE ONE NOR ANY OF THE OTHERS - - HAVE YOU NO OTHER SON?

WHY YES, THERE'S DAVID! - HE'S TEND- ING THE SHEEP!

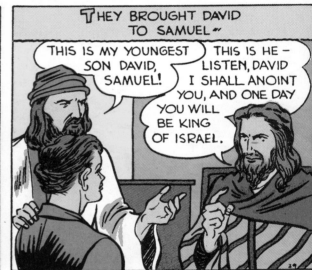

THEY BROUGHT DAVID TO SAMUEL ~

THIS IS MY YOUNGEST SON DAVID, SAMUEL!

THIS IS HE - LISTEN, DAVID I SHALL ANOINT YOU, AND ONE DAY YOU WILL BE KING OF ISRAEL.

YOU ARE ANOINTED, DAVID, AND THE SPIRIT OF THE LORD WILL BE ON YOU - GO BACK AND TEND YOUR SHEEP - WHEN THE TIME COMES FOR YOU TO BECOME KING, YOU WILL BE TOLD WHAT TO DO!

YES, SAMUEL, BUT NOW I'LL GO BACK AND CARE FOR MY LAMBS - WHEN CALLED, I SHALL BE READY!

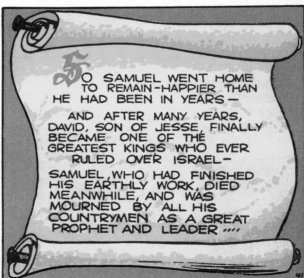

SO SAMUEL WENT HOME TO REMAIN - HAPPIER THAN HE HAD BEEN IN YEARS -

AND AFTER MANY YEARS, DAVID, SON OF JESSE, FINALLY BECAME ONE OF THE GREATEST KINGS WHO EVER RULED OVER ISRAEL -

SAMUEL, WHO HAD FINISHED HIS EARTHLY WORK, DIED MEANWHILE, AND WAS MOURNED BY ALL HIS COUNTRYMEN AS A GREAT PROPHET AND LEADER ~

THE STORY OF SAUL

THE FIRST KING OF ISRAEL

FROM FIRST SAMUEL, CHAPTERS 9-15.

SAUL THE SON OF KISH, WAS A FINE YOUNG MAN, TALLER THAN ANY OF THE PEOPLE OF HIS TRIBE ---

WHEN SAUL'S FATHER MISSED SOME OF HIS DONKEYS, HE ASKED HIS SON TO FIND THEM — SO SAUL AND A SERVANT STARTED TO SEARCH EVERYWHERE THROUGH THE SURROUNDING COUNTRY ---

WE MUST FIND THOSE ANIMALS — YOUR FATHER IS WORRIED ABOUT THEM!

WE HAVE GONE PAST MOUNT EPHRAIM, SHALISHA AND SHALIM — I GROW WEARY —

OVER THERE IS ZUPH, WHERE THE GREAT PROPHET SAMUEL LIVES!

PERHAPS HE CAN HELP US!

TELL US, DOES THE GREAT SEER LIVE IN ZUPH?

MAKE HASTE TO THE HIGH PLACE, FOR SAMUEL HAS INVITED MANY PEOPLE TO THE FEAST THERE!

ON THE WAY

HERE COMES SOMEONE WHO MAY KNOW WHERE SAMUEL IS — LET'S ASK HIM!

HAIL TO THEE!

WHY DO YOU HAIL ME?

BECAUSE YOU ARE THE MAN WHOM THE LORD HAS APPOINTED TO RULE OVER ISRAEL!

WHY, HE MUST BE SAMUEL THE SEER HIMSELF!

GO UP BEFORE ME TO THE HIGH PLACE, AND YOU SHALL EAT WITH ME TODAY!

WE ARE HUNGRY! WE HAVE NO BREAD, AND ONLY A FOURTH PART OF A SHEKEL OF SILVER LEFT!

DON'T FORGET TO ASK HIM ABOUT THE DONKEYS!

DON'T WORRY ABOUT THE LOST DONKEYS—THEY HAVE ALREADY BEEN FOUND AND RETURNED TO YOUR FATHER!

YOU RECOGNIZED ME AT ONCE AND I KNOW YOU TO BE WORTHY OF YOUR TITLE OF SEER!

THE OTHERS I INVITED ARE ALREADY HERE!

I AM HONORED!

SAMUEL LEADS HIS GUESTS TO THE PARLOR WHERE THE OTHERS ARE ASSEMBLED, WAITING ---

YOU AND YOUR FRIEND, SIT IN THE PLACE OF HONOR!

YOU ARE VERY KIND!

COOK, BRING ON OUR FOOD THAT WE MAY EAT!

YES, SIRE!

IT IS GOOD OF SAMUEL TO HONOR ME LIKE THIS!

FRIEND, SAMUEL IS A VERY GOOD MAN!

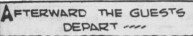

AFTERWARD THE GUESTS DEPART ----

I BID YOU GOODNIGHT, FOR SAUL AND MYSELF WILL RETIRE TOGETHER TO THE ROOF TOP OF MY HOUSE!

A BEAUTIFUL NIGHT, SAMUEL!

ONE ONLY THE LORD COULD CREATE!

THE NEXT MORNING, SAMUEL, SAUL AND THE SERVANT WALKED TOGETHER INTO THE COUNTRY---

YOU GO ON AHEAD I WOULD CONVERSE WITH SAUL A LITTLE BEFORE WE PART!

WONDER WHAT HE WANTS TO SAY?

YOU, SAUL, ARE THE CHOSEN ONE! - ABIDE BY THE WORDS OF GOD, AND YOU SHALL WIN GREAT GLORY!

I ANOINT YOU, SAUL, TO BE CAPTAIN OF THE LORD -- WE'LL MEET AGAIN IN MIZPEH!

LATER

COME, LET US OBEY SAMUEL AND GO TO MIZPEH!

SAMUEL WENT AHEAD TO MIZPEH AND WAS THERE WHEN SAUL AND HIS SERVANT ARRIVED---

LOOK AT THE PEOPLE HURRYING- THEY'RE GOING TO SEE SAMUEL, I THINK!

WE SHALL MEET THE SEER AGAIN VERY SHORTLY HERE!

I SHALL GIVE YOU A MAN WHO SHALL BECOME YOUR FIRST KING AND DO GREAT DEEDS!

SAUL RUNS AWAY TO HIDE...

WE SHALL FIND THIS MAN! HE SHALL BE BROUGHT UP HERE! — HE IS A BENJAMINITE!

WHY IS SAUL RUNNING?

THERE IS THE MAN!

I DO NOT DESERVE SUCH HONORS!

IT IS SAMUEL'S WISH — COME!

HE IS THE MAN! — THE SON OF KISH!

SEE WHOM THE LORD HAS CHOSEN!

AND ALL THE PEOPLE SHOUTED!

GOD SAVE THE KING!

YES, HE SHALL BE YOUR KING — THERE IS NO ONE LIKE HIM AMONG ALL THE PEOPLE!

AND SO FROM HUNTING HIS FATHER'S DONKEYS, SAUL WAS LED BY SAMUEL TO BE PROCLAIMED AS THE FIRST KING OVER THE ISRAELITES! — THUS DO SMALL ACTS LEAD TO GREAT THINGS, AND SAUL'S STAR ROSE THAT DAY SO THAT HE BECAME FAMOUS THROUGH ALL THE NATION OF ISRAEL

WE PART, BUT I SHALL NEVER FORGET

AS KING YOU WILL DO MANY MIGHTY DEEDS!

I SERVE A ROYAL MASTER— AND HAVE DINED WITH THE GREAT PROPHET, SAMUEL!

JUST ABOUT THEN THE AMMONITES INVADED ISRAEL, BUT SAUL WAS QUITE EQUAL TO THE OCCASION—

FOLLOW ME TO VICTORY! WE SHALL CRUSH THE INVADERS!

HAIL, KING SAUL!—HE WILL BRING VICTORY!

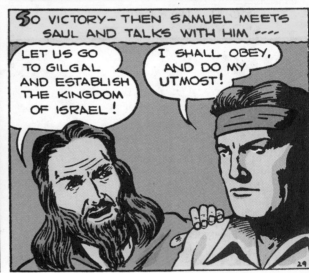

SO VICTORY—THEN SAMUEL MEETS SAUL AND TALKS WITH HIM—

LET US GO TO GILGAL AND ESTABLISH THE KINGDOM OF ISRAEL!

I SHALL OBEY, AND DO MY UTMOST!

WE SHALL MAKE SAUL KING!

WE ALL SHALL REJOICE OVER THE CHOICE OF THIS MAN!

SPEAK, SAUL!— IT IS YOUR TURN NOW, FOR THE PEOPLE ARE WILLING, AND WILL LISTEN TO YOUR WORDS!

SAUL! SPEAK TO US NOW!

SAMUEL HAS TOLD YOU TO FEAR AND SERVE THE LORD AND TO OBEY HIS VOICE!

NOW STAND STILL AND SEE THIS GREAT THING THE LORD WILL DO BEFORE YOUR EYES!

SAMUEL HAS CALLED UPON THE LORD TO SEND RAIN AND THUNDER AS A SIGN THIS DAY!

SO IT THUNDERED AND RAINED, HEAVILY ---

PRAY THAT WE DO NOT DIE!

FEAR NOT - THE RAIN HAS GONE! BUT SERVE THE LORD WITH ALL YOUR HEART, AND TURN NOT ASIDE!

SAUL WAS KING A YEAR, WHEN THE PHILISTINES RAIDED ISRAEL, GATHERING AN IMMENSE ARMY AT GEBA, 30,000 CHARIOTS, 6,000 HORSE AND SOLDIERS UNCOUNTABLE AS THE SANDS OF THE BEACH ---

THE YEARS PASS — THE WARS DRAG ON, BUT NOW SAUL HAS A SON, JONATHAN, TO HELP HIM ——

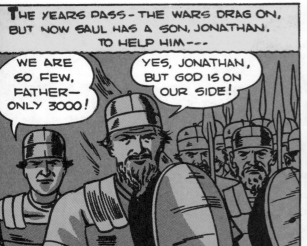

WE ARE SO FEW, FATHER — ONLY 3000!

YES, JONATHAN, BUT GOD IS ON OUR SIDE!

FROM THE RANKS, SAUL'S SON JONATHAN AND AN ARMOR-BEARER GO FORTH UNKNOWN TO SAUL ——

WE SHALL ENGAGE THE ENEMY NOW!

CAREFUL, JONATHAN!

I HAVE DOWNED TWENTY!

I HEAR THE OTHERS COMING TO OUR RESCUE!

SAUL'S ISRAELITES FINALLY CAME UP AND THE PHILISTINES WERE BEATEN FROM THE FIELD ——

YOU ARE A HERO TODAY, JONATHAN!

A GREAT VICTORY THIS DAY!

SO SAUL, AS KING OF ISRAEL FOUGHT MANY ENEMIES, AMONG THEM THE MOABITES, THE AMMONITES, THE AMA-LEKITES AND AGAIN THE PHILISTINES

YOUR KINGDOM IS STRENGTHENED — I HAVE KILLED THE KING OF THE AMALEKITES, AGAG — AND NOW, SAUL, WE SHALL PART!

SAUL SITS ON HIS THRONE ——— AND SPEAKS TO HIS SERVANT OF EARLIER DAYS ——

WE HAVE COME A FAR DISTANCE, MAN! — MY FATHER FOUND HIS LOST BEASTS, AND I HAVE FOUND A KINGDOM!

ISRAEL IS PROUD OF YOU, KING SAUL!

END

The Story of DAVID
PART ONE

FROM THE FIRST BOOK OF SAMUEL, STARTING AT CHAPTER 16

KING SAUL OF ISRAEL WAS TROUBLED IN SPIRIT AND HIS SERVANTS SUGGESTED A REMEDY---

WHAT IS THERE TO RELIEVE MY MIND?

A HARP PLAYER, SIRE!-WE SHALL SEEK ONE!

THERE IS THE SON OF JESSE THE BETHLEHEMITE, A GOOD AND HANDSOME YOUTH, WHO TENDS HIS FATHER'S SHEEP — WE GO TO CALL HIM TO PLAY FOR YOU—

AND DAVID CAME TO SAUL AND STOOD BEFORE HIM---

DOES MY MUSIC HELP YOU, SIRE?

I FEEL MUCH BETTER — I AM REFRESHED AGAIN!

A MESSENGER ENTERS---

THE PHILISTINES HAVE GATHERED ARMIES AT SHOCHOH TO WAR UPON ISRAEL!

THEN I GO TO PITCH OUR TENTS IN THE VALLEY OF ELAH!

IN THE MEANTIME DAVID HAD RETURNED TO CARE FOR HIS FATHER'S SHEEP----

THE PHILISTINES STOOD ON ONE MOUNTAIN SIDE, AS THE ISRAELITES CAME TO THE OPPOSITE MOUNTAINSIDE, WITH A VALLEY BETWEEN ----

HO! - I AM GOLIATH OF GATH COME TO CHALLENGE YOU TO BATTLE!

I DEFY ISRAEL! CHOOSE ONE OF YOUR MEN TO FIGHT ME — IF HE WINS, WE SURRENDER — IF I WIN, YOU SURRENDER!

IN THE CAMP OF THE ISRAELITES ---

HE IS SO BIG AND STRONG!

WE HAVE NO ONE TO FIGHT SUCH A MAN!

DAVID'S THREE BROTHERS ARE IN SAUL'S ARMY — THEIR FATHER IS WORRIED ABOUT THEM ---

GO TO YOUR BROTHERS AT THE BATTLE-FRONT — TAKE THIS BREAD, CHEESE AND PARCHED CORN AND BRING ME NEWS!

AND DAVID ROSE UP EARLY IN THE MORNING AND TOOK FOOD AND WENT TO FIND HIS BROTHERS

AT CAMP, DAVID RUNS TO HIS BROTHERS ---

HO! - OUR YOUNGEST BROTHER! - HOPE HE'S GOT SOMETHING GOOD! TO EAT!

BUT AT THAT MOMENT THEY ARE DISTURBED BY A SHOUT FROM THE VALLEY~~~

IS THERE NOT A MAN IN ISRAEL WHO CAN FIGHT? I DEFY ALL OF YOU!

SEE! IT IS GOLIATH—WHO CAN KILL HIM?

PERHAPS I MAY HELP YOU!

DAVID WANTS TO FIGHT GOLIATH—KING SAUL HEARS OF THIS AND SENDS FOR DAVID~~~

YOU NO LONGER NEED FEAR, OH KING!—WITH GOD'S HELP I WILL FIGHT AND SLAY THIS PHILISTINE!

BUT YOU ARE SO YOUNG AND NOT A SOLDIER!

ONCE A LION AND A BEAR ATTACKED MY SHEEP, AND I KILLED THEM BOTH— I CAN SLAY THIS GIANT GOLIATH WHO DEFIES YOUR ARMIES!

I WILL GIVE YOU MY ARMOR AND MY SPEAR~~~

THANKS, I DON'T WANT THEM— I WILL TAKE ONLY MY STAFF AND MY SLING SHOT!

DAVID GOES FORWARD~~~

AM I A DOG THAT YOU COME AT ME WITH A STICK? BEWARE, FOR I SHALL GIVE YOUR FLESH TO THE FOWLS OF THE AIR!

DAVID PICKS UP FIVE SMOOTH STONES FROM A BROOK~~~

YOU COME WITH A SPEAR, BUT I COME IN THE NAME OF THE LORD— I WILL SMITE YOU AND CUT OFF YOUR HEAD!

DAVID ATTACKS GOLIATH WITH STONE AND SLING

THE STONE HITS THE GIANT AND KNOCKS HIM DOWN

THEN DAVID RUNS UP TO GOLIATH, AND WITH GOLIATH'S OWN SWORD CUTS OFF HIS HEAD ~

HOW THE PHILISTINES RAN AWAY AFTER YOU KILLED GOLIATH!

WITH ONLY A SLINGSHOT, TOO!

I AM JONATHAN, SAUL'S SON. I'LL BE YOUR FRIEND FOR LIFE!

THEY SWORE TO BE LIKE BROTHERS FOR LIFE ~

TO PROVE MY FRIENDSHIP, I'LL GIVE YOU MY COAT, MY SWORD AND BOW!

YOUR FATHER, KING SAUL, HAS ASKED ME TO LIVE WITH YOU—

KING SAUL SPEAKS ~

DAVID IS A HERO! I APPOINT HIM TO BE THE HEAD OF ALL MY SOLDIERS!

AFTERWARD, THE ISRAELITES MARCHED HOME AND WERE DULY WELCOMED ~~~

THE WOMEN SING DAVID'S PRAISES ---

SAUL HAS SLAIN HIS THOUSANDS - BUT DAVID HIS TEN THOUSANDS! ♪♫

SAUL DOESN'T LIKE THIS ---

WHAT IS THIS? THEY PRAISE ME — BUT THEY PRAISE DAVID MORE — NEXT THING, HE'LL BE WANTING MY THRONE!

FROM THEN ON, KING SAUL EYED DAVID WITH SUSPICION. ONE DAY HIS JEALOUSY BURST BOUNDS, AND HE THREW A JAVELIN - BUT DAVID ESCAPED ---

THOUGH IN DANGER, DAVID BEHAVED HIMSELF WISELY — AND THE LORD WAS WITH HIM ---

SAUL THINKS TO HIMSELF ---

I SHALL DESTROY DAVID, LEST HE GRASP MY POWER, — I'LL OFFER HIM MERAB MY ELDER DAUGHTER AS HIS WIFE — THEN I'LL SEND HIM TO WAR — PERHAPS THE PHILISTINES WILL KILL HIM!

I NOW OFFER YOU MY ELDER DAUGHTER, MERAB, DAVID, TO BE YOUR WIFE, AND I COMMISSION YOU TO PROCEED AT ONCE TO COMBAT THE PHILISTINES!

DAVID FOLLOWED THE WISHES OF KING SAUL WITHOUT COMMENT ---

PREPARE TO MARCH, MEN — THE PHILISTINES ARE MARAUDING! AGAIN!

DOES DAVID KNOW MERAB ALREADY IS BETROTHED TO ANOTHER AND SAUL MERELY FOOLED HIM?

WHEN DAVID IS ABOUT TO LEAVE SAUL, A SERVANT SPEAKS TO THE KING ~~~

YOU MUST OFFER YOUR YOUNGER DAUGHTER, O KING, FOR MICHAL WHO SAW DAVID WHEN HE CAME HOME FROM SLAYING GOLIATH HAS COME TO LOVE HIM!

BRING DAVID TO ME BEFORE HE LEAVES

MY YOUNGER DAUGHTER MICHAL LOVES YOU, DAVID— I WILL GIVE HER TO YOU AS YOUR WIFE IF YOU WILL SLAY ME A HUNDRED PHILISTINES!

I'LL DO IT!

AND DAVID SLEW 200 MEN SHORTLY AFTERWARD, AND RETURNED HOME ~~~

LATER

NOW I KEEP MY PLEDGE— MICHAL WILL WED DAVID!

AND SOON THEREAFTER, DAVID TOOK MICHAL AS HIS WIFE ~~~

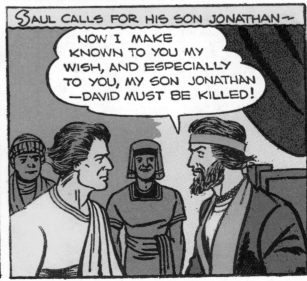

SAUL CALLS FOR HIS SON JONATHAN ~

NOW I MAKE KNOWN TO YOU MY WISH, AND ESPECIALLY TO YOU, MY SON JONATHAN —DAVID MUST BE KILLED!

BUT JONATHAN SEEKS DAVID----

DAVID, I HAVE REMEMBERED OUR PACT! - I COME TO ASK YOU TO FLEE! - MY FATHER SEEKS YOUR DEATH NOW!

I SHALL GO AT ONCE, MY FRIEND!

40

JONATHAN GOES BACK TO SAUL ---

WHY DO YOU WISH DAVID'S LIFE, FATHER? LET NOT THE KING SIN AGAINST ONE OF HIS LOYAL SERVANTS!

PERHAPS I HAVE BEEN HASTY, JONATHAN!

I SHALL ABIDE MY TIME, FOR EVEN MY SON DISTRUSTS ME!

AS THE LORD LIVES, DAVID SHALL NOT BE SLAIN!

JONATHAN, WHO KNEW WHERE DAVID WOULD GO, SOUGHT HIM OUT AT ONCE ---

DON'T BE AFRAID, DAVID - EVERYTHING IS ALL RIGHT— MY FATHER IS NO LONGER ANGRY WITH YOU!

YOU HAVE BEEN A TRUE FRIEND, JONATHAN, AND I WILL NOT FORGET!

45

The Story of DAVID — PART TWO

FROM THE FIRST BOOK OF SAMUEL, CHAP. 19 AND FOLLOWING CHAPTERS.

AND THERE WAS WAR AGAIN —AND DAVID WENT OUT AND FOUGHT WITH THE PHILISTINES, AND DEFEATED THEM WITH GREAT SLAUGHTER —AND THEY FLED FROM HIM ---

BUT KING SAUL WAS STILL JEALOUS OF DAVID'S GREAT VICTORIES ---

THREE TIMES HAVE I THROWN MY SPEAR AT DAVID —EACH TIME HE'S ESCAPED —BUT NEXT TIME!

DAVID GOES HOME TO HIS WIFE MICHAL, FEARING WHAT KING SAUL MAY DO NEXT ---

HE THREW A SPEAR AT ME AGAIN, MICHAL!

I'LL HELP YOU TO ESCAPE BEFORE MORNING!

AT SAUL'S PALACE ---

SEND MESSENGERS AND SPIES TO SURROUND DAVID'S HOUSE! —IF HE TRIES TO ESCAPE, KILL HIM!

WE'LL HAVE TO WATCH ALL NIGHT SO DAVID WON'T ESCAPE US!

IN DAVID'S HOUSE ---

I'LL LET YOU DOWN FROM THIS WINDOW —THEN RUN AWAY QUICKLY— THEY ARE NOT WATCHING THIS SIDE OF THE HOUSE!

PUT A PILLOW IN MY BED— THEY'LL THINK I'M STILL THERE!

IN THE MORNING KING SAUL'S MESSENGERS COME TO SEIZE DAVID ~~~

IN THE NAME OF THE KING WE SEEK DAVID!

HE IS SICK— YOU CANNOT DISTURB HIM!

A SECOND TIME KING SAUL SENT THE MESSENGERS TO TAKE DAVID ~~~

KING SAUL COMMANDS WE REMOVE THE BED WITH DAVID TO HIM!

COME THEN!

ONLY A PILLOW IN THE BED!—DAVID HAS ESCAPED US!

SAUL WILL BE VERY ANGRY!

KING SAUL RAGES IN HIS PALACE ~~~

BRING MICHAL, MY DAUGHTER, IMMEDIATELY!

YES, SIRE!

WHY HAVE YOU DECEIVED ME AND HELPED MY ENEMY ESCAPE?

I COULD NOT HELP IT— HE THREATENED ME!

MEANWHILE DAVID HAS FLED TO RAMAH WHERE LIVES SAMUEL THE PROPHET ~~~

COME IN AND TELL ME WHAT BRINGS YOU, DAVID?

I NEED HELP, SAMUEL!

I WILL TAKE YOU TO NAIOTH WITH ME—YOU WILL BE SAFE THERE FOR AWHILE!

SAUL'S SPIES LEARNED WHERE DAVID WAS, BUT WHEN THEY WERE SENT TO CAPTURE THE HERO, THEY SAW HIM WITH THE HOLY SAMUEL AND OTHER PROPHETS, AND WENT HOME — SAUL SENT NEW MESSENGERS AND SPIES, BUT THEY ALSO RETURNED EMPTY-HANDED! — SO SAUL, THE KING OF ISRAEL, HIMSELF CAME TO NAIOTH! BUT DAVID FLED FROM KING SAUL AND WENT TO SAUL'S SON, HIS FRIEND JONATHAN...

—AND JONATHAN, WHO LOVED DAVID AS HE LOVED HIS OWN SOUL, FOUND A WAY TO SAVE HIS FRIEND'S LIFE!

WHAT HAVE I DONE, JONATHAN? WHAT MAKES KING SAUL SEEK MY LIFE?

IS HE ANGRY AGAIN? — I DID NOT KNOW — I WILL HELP YOU!

WALKING IN A FIELD BEFORE PARTING, THE TWO FRIENDS TALK—

HIDE IN THE PLACE WHERE YOU HID ONCE BEFORE— REMAIN THREE DAYS — I SHALL COME WITH A BOY, SHOOT ARROWS AT THE ROCK, AND SEND THE BOY AFTER THEM. IF I CALL TO HIM THAT THE ARROWS ARE BETWEEN HIM AND ME, YOU ARE SAFE! IF I TELL HIM THE ARROWS LIE BEYOND HIM, YOU MUST FLEE!

THAT NIGHT, DAVID'S SEAT AT THE PALACE BANQUET TABLE WAS EMPTY — SAUL HOPES SOMETHING HAS HAPPENED TO HIM —

HMM—JONATHAN ALONE— WITHOUT DAVID—GOOD!

ON THE SECOND NIGHT OF DAVID'S ABSENCE, SAUL'S SUSPICIONS GROW —

JONATHAN, MY SON, WHERE IS DAVID?

HE ASKED LEAVE OF ME TO MEET HIS FAMILY IN BETHLEHEM!

DON'T YOU KNOW THAT AS LONG AS DAVID LIVES YOU WILL NEVER SUCCEED ME AS KING? — BRING HIM TO ME—HE MUST SURELY DIE!

JOHNATHAN SHOOTS ARROWS AND SENDS THE BOY AFTER THEM SO HE CAN CALL OUT THE SECRET MESSAGE TO DAVID ---

NOT THERE, BOY, LOOK BEYOND YOU -- **BEYOND!**

JONATHAN SENDS THE BOY AWAY AND BIDS DAVID FAREWELL AS THEY RENEW THEIR SINCERE PLEDGE OF FRIENDSHIP ---

I AM YOUR TRUE FRIEND, DAVID, EVEN THOUGH MY FATHER HATES ME BECAUSE OF YOU!

DAVID IS HUNGRY AND ALSO NEEDS A WEAPON - HE GOES TO A PRIEST, AHIMELECH, WHO GIVES HIM BREAD AND THE SWORD WITH WHICH DAVID HIMSELF HAD KILLED GOLIATH, MANY YEARS BEFORE ~

FAREWELL, AHIMELECH! I GO ON SECRET BUSINESS WHICH IS URGENT!

UNKNOWN TO DAVID AND THE PRIEST ----

HA! - I, DOEG THE EDOMITE, WILL REPORT WHAT I HAVE SEEN AND HEARD THIS DAY! - SAUL WILL REWARD ME!

AFTER A WHILE, DAVID FLED TO THE CAVE OF ADULLAM - MEN OF HIS FAMILY AND MEN WHO WERE OPPRESSED JOINED HIM ----

WE ARE 400 NOW, DAVID!

I HAVE SOME BUSINESS — THEN WE FLEE TO JUDAH, INTO THE FOREST OF HARETH AND MAKE A STAND!

YOU ARE OUR CAPTAIN, DAVID!

IN SAUL'S PALACE ----

WHAT IS THIS? - SPEAK UP, DOEG!

I SAW DAVID — I TELL YOU THE PRIEST AHIMELECH HELPED HIM!

DOEG, FIND AHIMELECH WHOM I SHALL ACCUSE OF TREACHERY! — SLAY HIM AND OTHER PRIESTS WHO AID DAVID!

A YOUNG PRIEST RUNS UP TO DAVID IN THE FOREST —

I AM ABIATHAR, SON OF AHIMELECH WHO BEFRIENDED YOU! — DOEG, SAUL'S SPY, HAS KILLED MY FATHER AND MANY OTHERS!

I GRIEVE FOR YOUR FATHER — STAY HERE WITH ME — YOU WILL BE SAFE!

WHEN NEWS CAME OF A PHILISTINE ATTACK AGAIN, DAVID ASKED GOD IF HE WAS TO GO AND FIGHT THEM —

GO AND SMITE THE PHILISTINES, BESIEGING KEILAH — I WILL DELIVER YOUR ENEMIES TO YOU!

WHEN KING SAUL LEARNED THAT DAVID HAD FOUGHT AND WON AND WAS IN KEILAH, HE ORDERED THE CITY BESIEGED —

DAVID REMAINS IN KEILAH — SEND AN ARMY THERE! — WALLS SURROUND THE TOWN AND HE CANNOT GET AWAY!

KING SAUL'S ARMY APPROACHES TO GET DAVID —

DAVID, SIRE! — AN ISRAELITE ARMY APPROACHES, WITH KING SAUL AT THE HEAD! — THEY COME TO CAPTURE YOU!!

WE MUST FLEE — I GO FIRST AND ALONE!

SAUL'S MEN SURROUND KEILAH — TOO LATE!

IF YOU'RE LOOKING FOR DAVID, YOU'VE COME TOO LATE — HE AND HIS MEN HAVE GONE!

NOW DAVID WENT TO THE MOUNTAIN WILDERNESS OF ZIPH, WHILE SAUL DAILY PURSUED AND SEARCHED FOR HIM THERE ----

JONATHAN, KING SAUL'S SON, SECRETLY VISITS DAVID IN THE FOREST ----

THE HAND OF MY FATHER SHALL NEVER TOUCH YOU, DAVID, I PROMISE!

THE MEN OF THE HILLS GO TO KING SAUL ----

WE CAN LEAD YOU TO THIS DAVID, SIRE!

HE'S AT THE HILL OF HACHILAH! --THAT'S SOUTHWARD OF JESHIMON!

BUT DAVID, INFORMED OF THE TREACHERY, MOVED TO MAON IN THE WILDERNESS AND WAS NOT CAUGHT!

I CAN SEE SAUL'S MEN SEARCHING ON THAT OPPOSITE HILLSIDE!

ONE DAY WHILE SEARCHING FOR DAVID, SAUL BECAME WEARY AND LAY DOWN TO REST IN A CAVE ----

I SHALL SLEEP A LITTLE, THEN JOIN THE OTHERS!

LATER- DAVID FINDS SAUL ASLEEP THERE- ALONE!

KING SAUL!- BUT I WILL NOT HURT HIM - I WILL ONLY CUT OFF A PIECE OF HIS ROBE AND GO!

LATER

MY ROBE CUT! - THIS IS STRANGE!

AS SAUL LEAVES, DAVID RUNS TO HIM ---

SAUL! MY LORD THE KING!!

DAVID!

IT WAS I WHO CUT YOUR ROBE - YOU WERE IN MY POWER AS YOU LAY THERE ASLEEP, BUT I DIDN'T WANT TO HURT YOU! THOUGH YOU SEEK MY LIFE, I WOULD NOT RAISE MY HAND AGAINST MY KING - NOW WILL YOU BELIEVE ME, SIRE?

YOU ARE BETTER THAN I, DAVID - FOR I HAVE DONE EVIL TO YOU AND YOU HAVE REWARDED ME WITH GOOD!

7

NOW I KNOW THAT ONE DAY YOU WILL REIGN AS KING OVER ISRAEL - BUT DO NO HARM TO MY SON JONATHAN!

ARE NOT HE AND I SWORN BROTHERS? AND NOW THAT YOU AND I ARE FRIENDS AGAIN, I SHALL BE HAPPY!!

THE STORY OF DAVID KING OF ISRAEL

PART THREE

FROM FIRST AND SECOND BOOKS OF SAMUEL AND THE FIRST BOOK OF KINGS

THOUGH DAVID, THE HERO OF ISRAEL, HAS TWICE SPARED THE LIFE OF KING SAUL, THE KING IS NOT GRATEFUL—HE STILL WANTS TO DESTROY DAVID, THE NATIONAL HERO, OF WHOSE POWER HE IS AFRAID ——

THIS TIME DAVID SHALL NOT ESCAPE ME!

KING SAUL IS OPENLY FRIENDLY, BUT FOR HOW LONG?—SOME DAY I SHALL PERISH AT HIS HAND—IT IS BETTER TO FLEE TO THE LAND OF THE PHILISTINES, SAUL'S ENEMIES—THERE I CAN TAKE REFUGE AND SAUL WILL NOT SEEK ME ANY MORE!

SO DAVID WITH SIX HUNDRED FOLLOWERS WENT INTO THE PHILISTINES' COUNTRY ——

BRING YOUR FAMILIES AND WE WILL MARCH TO KING ACHISH OF GATH IN THE LAND OF THE PHILISTINES!

KING ACHISH RECEIVES DAVID AND GIVES HIM A CITY FOR HIMSELF AND HIS FOLLOWERS ——

IF I HAVE FOUND FAVOR IN YOUR SIGHT, GIVE ME A PLACE WHERE I AND MY PEOPLE MAY DWELL!

I WILL GIVE YOU THE CITY OF ZIKLAG, DAVID!

THE PHILISTINES PREPARE TO MAKE WAR AGAINST THEIR OLD ENEMY KING SAUL OF ISRAEL—KING ACHISH WANTS DAVID TO FIGHT AGAINST KING SAUL AND DAVID'S OWN PEOPLE—HOWEVER, THE PRINCES OF THE PHILISTINES ARE AFRAID OF DAVID —

DON'T LET DAVID GO TO BATTLE WITH US, O KING!—HOW DO WE KNOW HE WON'T TURN ON US?

As DAVID RETURNED TO ZIKLAG, HE FOUND THE AMALEKITES HAD RAIDED IT IN HIS ABSENCE, AND CARRIED AWAY THE WOMEN AND CHILDREN AS CAPTIVES. HE PURSUED AND KILLED THE AMALEKITES AND RESCUED THE WOMEN AND CHILDREN.

MEANWHILE, A FURIOUS BATTLE WAS RAGING BETWEEN THE PHILISTINES AND KING SAUL'S ARMIES - SAUL WAS LOSING

THE BATTLE GOES AGAINST ME! JONATHAN AND MY OTHER TWO SONS ARE SLAIN AND I AM SORELY WOUNDED!

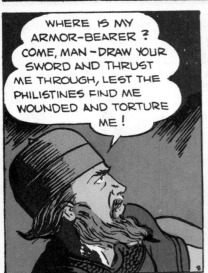

WHERE IS MY ARMOR-BEARER? COME, MAN - DRAW YOUR SWORD AND THRUST ME THROUGH, LEST THE PHILISTINES FIND ME WOUNDED AND TORTURE ME!

THE ARMOR-BEARER REFUSED TO KILL HIS KING

I WOULD NOT KILL MY KING! - HE HIMSELF HAS FALLEN ON HIS SWORD!

TO DAVID AT ZIKLAG CAME A MAN WHO HAD ESCAPED FROM THE BATTLE - HE TOLD OF THE DEATH OF SAUL AND JONATHAN

I GRIEVE FOR SAUL AND JONATHAN - HOW THE MIGHTY HAVE FALLEN!

DAVID SPEAKS TO HIS MEN ---

THE LORD HAS DIRECTED ME TO GO TO HEBRON - I KNOW NOW, WITH SAUL DEAD, I SHALL BE MADE KING!

BUT THE ISRAELITES WERE DIVIDED, AND JUDAH WAS SEPARATED FROM ISRAEL, NOW RULED BY ISH-BOSHETH, A SON OF SAUL. DAVID RULED OVER JUDAH ---

I, ABNER, SWEAR TO BRING ISH-BOSHETH AND ALL ISRAEL TO YOUR RULE, DAVID!

BUT ABNER IS MURDERED BY JOAB WHO MIS-TRUSTED HIM AND WISHES REVENGE ---

DIE FOR DECEIVING DAVID AND FOR KILLING MY BROTHER IN BATTLE!

AND A SHORT TIME AFTER THAT KING ISH-BOSHETH IS KILLED BY HIS OWN MEN AS HE SLEEPS ----

THE KING IS DEAD—BAANAH AND RECHAB, CAPTAINS OF OUR GUARD, DID IT AS ISH-BOSHETH WAS LYING ON HIS BED!

SO THE TRIBES OF ISRAEL CAME TO ANOINT DAVID OVER ISRAEL—THUS UNITED, THE ISRAELITE ARMIES, LED BY DAVID, TRIUMPHED OVER THE PHILISTINES ---

HAIL TO KING DAVID—HE LED US TO CONQUER THE PHILISTINES!

NOW WE ARE UNCONQUERABLE!

AND YEARS PASSED - DAVID WAS A GREAT KING AND HAD A SON ABSALOM, WHOM HE LOVED VERY MUCH ---

THE PEOPLE LOVE ME BETTER THAN KING DAVID, MY FATHER—WHY SHOULD I NOT BE KING?-I'LL SEND WORD TO THE TRIBES OF ISRAEL THAT WHEN THE TRUMPET SOUNDS, THEY WILL ALL CRY, ABSALOM REIGNETH AS KING IN HEBRON!

16

A MESSENGER COMES TO KING DAVID ---

ABSALOM, YOUR SON, HAS REBELLED AGAINST YOU AND SEIZED HEBRON! NOW HE MARCHES AGAINST YOU WITH A STRONG FORCE!

WE MUST LEAVE THE CITY OF JERUSALEM BEFORE ABSALOM OVERTAKES US!-OH, MUST I FIGHT AGAINST MY OWN SON!

THEN IT CAME TO PASS THAT DAVID'S AND ABSALOM'S ARMIES MET IN THE WOOD OF EPHRAIM ----

WE MUST TEACH ABSALOM HIS LESSON!

THE BATTLE'S GOING AGAINST ME - I MUST GET AWAY AT ONCE!

RIDING ON A DONKEY, ABSALOM FLEES ---

FASTER, FASTER BEAST, I MUST ESCAPE MY FATHER'S MEN!

ABSALOM'S HAIR CATCHES ON AN OVER-HANGING BRANCH OF A GREAT OAK TREE ---

AH -I, JOAB, WILL PUT THREE DARTS THROUGH THE HEART OF ABSALOM, HUNG TO THAT TREE!

HA! -NOW I WILL TELL DAVID THAT THE REBELLION IS FULLY CRUSHED!

DAVID IS GRIEF-STRICKEN AT ABSALOM'S DEATH ~~

OH, MY SON ABSALOM! MY SON, MY SON! WOULD GOD I HAD DIED INSTEAD OF YOU!

AFTERWARDS THERE WERE THREE YEARS OF FAMINE — DAVID INQUIRES OF THE LORD THE REASON ~~~

I HAVE SENT THE FAMINE BECAUSE OF THE EVIL DONE BY THE HOUSE OF SAUL — MAKE ATONEMENT!

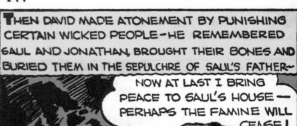

THEN DAVID MADE ATONEMENT BY PUNISHING CERTAIN WICKED PEOPLE — HE REMEMBERED SAUL AND JONATHAN, BROUGHT THEIR BONES AND BURIED THEM IN THE SEPULCHRE OF SAUL'S FATHER~

NOW AT LAST I BRING PEACE TO SAUL'S HOUSE — PERHAPS THE FAMINE WILL CEASE!

THE FAMINE DID CEASE, BUT THE PHILISTINES RAIDED AGAIN!

DAVID'S ARMIES ATTACKED THE PHILISTINES ~~~

THE LORD IS MY ROCK AND MY FORTRESS AND MY DELIVERER — I WILL CALL ON THE LORD — SO SHALL I BE SAVED FROM MY ENEMIES!

DAVID PRAYED AND ISRAEL TRIUMPHED ~~~

IN MY DISTRESS I CALLED UPON THE LORD, AND HE DID HEAR MY VOICE! — HE DELIVERED ME FROM MY STRONG ENEMY AND FROM THEM THAT HATED ME!

NO ONE CAN DEFEAT DAVID!

EVEN IN HIS OLD AGE, DAVID WINS OUR WARS!

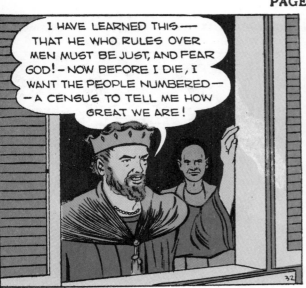

I HAVE LEARNED THIS —— THAT HE WHO RULES OVER MEN MUST BE JUST, AND FEAR GOD! — NOW BEFORE I DIE, I WANT THE PEOPLE NUMBERED —— A CENSUS TO TELL ME HOW GREAT WE ARE!

SO JOAB, NOW CAPTAIN OF ISRAEL'S ARMIES, WENT OUT AND TOOK A CENSUS, AND IN NINE MONTHS AND TWENTY DAYS HE RETURNED TO JERUSALEM ——

THE PEOPLE OF ISRAEL ARE EIGHT HUNDRED THOUSAND, AND OF JUDAH, FIVE HUNDRED THOUSAND!

AFTERWARD GAD, A HOLY MAN OF ISRAEL, WENT TO DAVID WITH A MESSAGE ——

NOW BUILD A GREAT ALTAR TO GOD ON THE THRESHING FLOOR OF ARAUNAH THE JEBUSITE!

I OBEY, FOR YOU SPEAK FOR THE LORD OUR GOD — I SHALL GO AT ONCE!

DAVID GOES TO THE THRESHING PLACE ——

I, ARAUNAH, WELCOME YOU! WHY HAVE YOU COME TO ME, KING DAVID?

— TO BUY THIS PLACE OF YOU TO BUILD AN ALTAR TO THE LORD OUR GOD!

TAKE IT, AND OFFER WHAT SEEMS GOOD AND FAIR TO YOU —— AND GOD BLESS YOU!

SO DAVID BUILT AN ALTAR ——— ONE OF HIS LAST DEEDS TO THE GLORY OF GOD ——

THIS WAS BUILT BY DAVID, AND GOD WAS PLEASED!

FOR FORTY YEARS DAVID HAS RULED US NOW!

NOW DAVID KNEW HIS END WAS NEAR, AND HE CALLED SOLOMON, HIS SON TO HIM ---

MY SON, SOLOMON, I GO THE WAY OF ALL THE EARTH - BE A STRONG KING AND SHOW YOURSELF A MAN - WALK IN THE WAYS OF THE LORD AND KEEP HIS COMMANDMENTS!

I WILL, FATHER, I WILL INCREASE GOD'S GLORY YEAR AFTER YEAR!

SO DAVID SLEPT WITH HIS FATHERS AND WAS BURIED IN THE CITY OF DAVID ---

OF ALL THE ONE HUNDRED AND FIFTY PSALMS IN THE BIBLE, THIS IS THE BEST KNOWN AND LOVED ---

A PSALM OF DAVID

THE **LORD** IS MY SHEPHERD: I SHALL NOT WANT.

2. HE MAKETH ME TO LIE DOWN IN GREEN PASTURES: HE LEADETH ME BESIDE THE STILL WATERS.

3. HE RESTORETH MY SOUL: HE LEADETH ME IN THE PATHS OF RIGHTEOUSNESS FOR HIS NAME'S SAKE.

4. YEA, THOUGH I WALK THROUGH THE VALLEY OF THE SHADOW OF DEATH, I WILL FEAR NO EVIL: FOR THOU ART WITH ME: THY ROD AND THY STAFF THEY COMFORT ME.

5. THOU PREPAREST A TABLE BEFORE ME IN THE PRESENCE OF MINE ENEMIES: THOU ANOINTEST MY HEAD WITH OIL; MY CUP RUNNETH OVER.

6. SURELY GOODNESS AND MERCY SHALL FOLLOW ME ALL THE DAYS OF MY LIFE: AND I WILL DWELL IN THE HOUSE OF THE **LORD** FOR EVER.

SOLOMON ASCENDS THE THRONE OF ISRAEL ---

I ASCEND A MIGHTY THRONE - BUT I WILL MAKE IT MIGHTIER! - IN REMEMBRANCE OF MY FATHER DAVID, ISRAEL SHALL BE GLORIOUS!

KING SOLOMON MARRIED THE DAUGHTER OF THE PHARAOH OR KING OF EGYPT AND SO TWO MIGHTY COUNTRIES WERE UNITED - AND THE PEOPLE KNEW SOLOMON FOR A WISE KING ---

MY FATHER UNITED THE LAND - I WIDEN IT BY ALLIANCE!

DAVID WAS A GREAT KING, BUT KING SOLOMON SHALL SURPASS HIM!

HE HAS WISDOM BUT HE IS AS HUMBLE AS A CHILD!

END

THE STORY OF SOLOMON

FROM THE BOOK OF FIRST KINGS

WHEN SOLOMON SUCCEEDED HIS FATHER DAVID, AS KING OF THE HEBREWS, HE WONDERED WHETHER HE HAD THE WISDOM TO CARRY ON DAVID'S WORK—

TO RULE MY PEOPLE WISELY—THAT'S WHAT I WANT MORE THAN LONG LIFE OR RICHES OR THE LIVES OF MY ENEMIES!

THE LORD APPEARED TO SOLOMON IN A DREAM, SAYING, "ASK WHAT SHALL I GIVE YOU!"

O LORD, GIVE ME AN UNDERSTANDING HEART TO JUDGE YOUR PEOPLE!

I WILL GIVE YOU A WISE AND UNDERSTANDING HEART—OBEY MY COMMANDMENTS AND YOU SHALL HAVE RICHES, GLORY AND LONG LIFE!

KING SOLOMON AWAKES AND BELIEVES THAT GOD SPOKE TO HIM IN A DREAM—

NO MATTER WHAT HAPPENS, I KNOW NOW THAT I SHALL BE GIVEN WISDOM!

KING SOLOMON IS PUT TO THE TEST OF JUDGING WISELY—

HERE ARE THE TWO WOMEN WHO WISH YOUR COUNSEL, SIRE!

WE LIVE IN THE SAME HOUSE, SIRE, AND WE EACH HAD A CHILD—BUT THIS WOMAN'S CHILD DIED, AND WHEN I SLEPT SHE PUT HER DEAD CHILD BESIDE ME, AND TOOK MINE FOR HERSELF—BUT I KNOW THE LIVING BOY IS MINE, THOUGH SHE CLAIMS IT!

By THIS WISE JUDGMENT, KING SOLOMON WON FAME FOR HIS WISDOM AND PEOPLE CAME FROM ALL NATIONS AND KINGS OF THE EARTH TO HEAR HIM — — THREE THOUSAND PROVERBS HE MADE, AND 1005 SONGS — HE HAD GREAT RICHES TOO, AND THOUSANDS OF HORSES FOR HIS CHARIOTS AND HIS HORSEMEN ---

GOD HAS BEEN GOOD TO ME — I WILL BUILD A TEMPLE HERE TO HIM — I'LL ASK KING HIRAM OF TYRE, MY FATHER'S FRIEND, FOR LUMBER!

HIRAM OF TYRE ANSWERS SOLOMON WITH ACTION! — SOON LUMBER GOES BY SEA TO KING SOLOMON ON FLOATS ---

WE GO TO SOLOMON WITH WOOD FOR HIS TEMPLE!

CEDAR WOOD AND FIR LOGS FROM KING HIRAM, DAVID'S FRIEND!

IN RETURN FOR THE LUMBER, I'LL GIVE HIRAM WHEAT AND OIL WHILE HE IS HELPING ME BUILD THE TEMPLE!

FROM ALL OVER ISRAEL, MEN CAME TO WORK ON THE TEMPLE ---

AN ARMY OF WORKERS! 70,000 MEN TO CARRY BURDENS, 80,000 TO HEW STONES!

I'VE MADE A LEAGUE OF PEACE WITH KING HIRAM OF TYRE, AS I DID WITH YOUR FATHER PHARAOH OF EGYPT WHEN I MARRIED YOU!

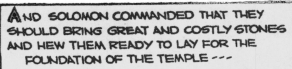

AND SOLOMON COMMANDED THAT THEY SHOULD BRING GREAT AND COSTLY STONES AND HEW THEM READY TO LAY FOR THE FOUNDATION OF THE TEMPLE ---

FOR FOUR YEARS MEN WORKED GATHERING MATERIAL FOR THE TEMPLE AND LAYING THE FOUNDATION ---

FOUR YEARS, AND ONLY NOW THEY'RE READY TO BUILD!

THIS WILL BE THE FINEST TEMPLE IN THE WORLD!

AFTER SEVEN LONG YEARS, THE LAST STONES WERE PUT INTO PLACE, AND THEN SOLOMON HELD A TWO WEEK CELEBRATION TO DEDICATE IT ---

NOW I WILL BRING INTO THE HOUSE OF THE LORD ALL THE SACRED VESSELS OF GOLD AND SILVER!

LORD GOD OF ISRAEL, THERE IS NO GOD LIKE THEE! - WE COME TODAY TO DEDICATE THIS WONDERFUL TEMPLE TO YOUR SERVICE!

NEAR THE COURT OF THE TEMPLE, SOLOMON BUILT A HOUSE FOR HIMSELF AND ONE FOR HIS WIFE ---

NOW I SHALL BUILD MANY GREAT CITIES IN ISRAEL!

YES, MY LORD, AND I WITH ALL THE PEOPLE BLESS YOU FOR WHAT YOU ARE DOING!

SO SOLOMON BUILT NEW CITIES, SUCH AS GEZER, BAALATH, TADMOR AND OTHERS ---

AND THEN KING SOLOMON BUILT A MIGHTY FLEET OF SHIPS, WITH A GREAT PORT AT EZION-GEBER ON THE RED SEA SHORE IN THE LAND OF EDOM ~~~

KING HIRAM OF TYRE IS TO SEND US PILOTS AND GUIDES FOR ISRAEL'S SEAMEN!

AT THE END OF TWENTY YEARS. SOLOMON AND HIRAM RENEWED THEIR ALLIANCE ~~~

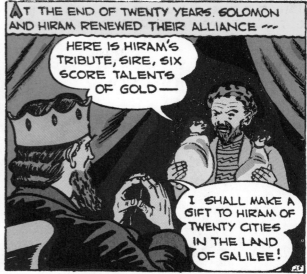

HERE IS HIRAM'S TRIBUTE, SIRE, SIX SCORE TALENTS OF GOLD—

I SHALL MAKE A GIFT TO HIRAM OF TWENTY CITIES IN THE LAND OF GALILEE!

THE QUEEN OF SHEBA, DOUBTING THE STORIES OF SOLOMON'S WISDOM, COMES TO TRY HIM WITH HARD QUESTIONS ~~~

SPICES AND GOLD AND PRECIOUS STONES FOR SOLOMON!

OUR QUEEN DOESN'T BELIEVE SOLOMON IS AS WISE AS THEY SAY!

ALL OF THE QUEEN OF SHEBA'S QUESTIONS WERE SO WELL ANSWERED BY SOLOMON THAT SHE DEPARTED SATISFIED ~~~

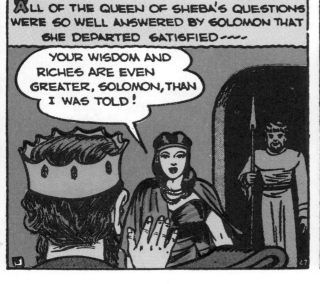

YOUR WISDOM AND RICHES ARE EVEN GREATER, SOLOMON, THAN I WAS TOLD!

SOON SOLOMON, IN ALL HIS GLORY, HAD BUILT A THRONE OF IVORY OVERLAID WITH GOLD ~~~

BUT THE TIME CAME WHEN SOLOMON FORGOT HIS PROMISE TO THE LORD, AND TURNED TO WORSHIP STRANGE GODS ----

YOU HAVE DISOBEYED ME! I WILL DIVIDE YOUR KINGDOM!

AND SO, AS SOLOMON TURNED AWAY FROM GOD, TROUBLES BEGAN TO CROP UP-- FIRST A REBELLION STARTED UNDER HADAD, THE EDOMITE.

THE KING OF EGYPT FAVORS ME! WE REVOLT AND RAID ISRAEL!

AND AS SOLOMON CONTINUED TO TAX HIS PEOPLE HEAVILY--MORE REBELLIONS FLARED UP..

ALSO REZON, AN EXILE, GATHERED BANDS TO RAID ISRAEL FROM DAMASCUS WHERE HE CAME TO RULE ----

EVEN JEROBOAM, A SERVANT OF SOLOMON, WAS PERSUADED TO RISE AGAINST THE KING ~~

BUT SOLOMON HAS MADE ME A GOVERNOR. WHY SHOULD I REBEL, AHIJAH?

BECAUSE SOLOMON HAS TURNED TO STRANGE GODS, THE KINGDOM WILL BE DIVIDED, AND YOU WILL ONE DAY BE KING OVER ISRAEL.

CAN THIS BE TRUE? WILL SOLOMON'S GLORY DESCEND TO ME?

BUT SOLOMON'S FULL PUNISHMENT WAS NOT TO COME YET— STILL IN POWER, HE SOUGHT TO KILL JEROBOAM, WHO FLED TO EGYPT

I HAVE REIGNED FORTY YEARS, MY SON REHOBOAM, AND MY LIFE IS NEARLY SPENT— YOU IT IS WHOM I APPOINT TO SUCCEED ME —

I SHALL TRY TO RULE AS GREATLY AS YOU, FATHER!

BUT FINALLY SOLOMON DIED, AND HIS SON REHOBOAM BECAME KING. RETURNED FROM EGYPT, JEROBOAM LEADS THE PEOPLE OF ISRAEL BEFORE REHOBOAM TO ASK FOR GREATER LENIENCY—

SOLOMON WAS HARD ON THE PEOPLE— THEY WILL SERVE YOU IF YOU ARE KIND!

COME AGAIN IN THREE DAYS!

THREE DAYS LATER—DISREGARDING HIS WISE COUNSELLORS, REHOBOAM REFUSES THE PEOPLE'S PLEAS—

MY FATHER MADE YOUR YOKE HEAVY, BUT I WILL MAKE IT HEAVIER!

WE DON'T HAVE TO SERVE YOU!

SO THE PEOPLE OF ISRAEL REVOLTED FROM REHOBOAM— THEY MADE JEROBOAM KING OVER ALL THE TRIBES OF ISRAEL BUT ONE — — THAT WAS JUDAH ~~~

YOU SHALL BE OUR KING!

LET SOLOMON'S SON REIGN ONLY OVER JUDAH!

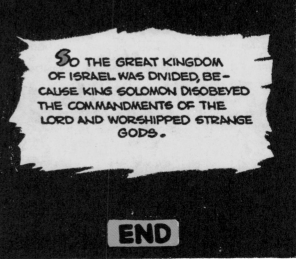

SO THE GREAT KINGDOM OF ISRAEL WAS DIVIDED, BE- CAUSE KING SOLOMON DISOBEYED THE COMMANDMENTS OF THE LORD AND WORSHIPPED STRANGE GODS.

END

The Story of ELIJAH

FROM THE FIRST BOOK
OF KINGS
CHAPTERS 16 THROUGH 22

TO THE LORD
GOD OF ISRAEL

AHAB, SEVENTH KING OF ISRAEL, TOOK AS A WIFE NOT ONE OF HIS OWN PEOPLE, BUT JEZEBEL, DAUGHTER OF THE KING OF TYRE ---

WHY COULDN'T HE MARRY AN ISRAELITE?

THEY SAY SHE WORSHIPS BAAL INSTEAD OF THE TRUE GOD!

JEZEBEL SOON BEGAN TO URGE HER HUSBAND TO WORSHIP THE SUN GOD ---

YOU DON'T LOVE ME AHAB, OR YOU'D DO WHAT I ASK!

WELL, THEN, I WILL! I'LL BUILD A TEMPLE TO BAAL - IN YOUR HONOR!

THOSE WHO WORSHIPPED THE TRUE GOD WERE PUNISHED ---

YOU WILL WORSHIP BAAL, NOT YOUR JEHOVAH — OR MORE WHIPPING!

WICKED QUEEN! WHIPS CAN'T CHANGE MEN'S MINDS!

ELIJAH, A MAN OF GOD, PROTESTED THESE EVILS TO THE KING ---

ELIJAH— WHAT IS IT? YOU'RE ANGRY!

YOU'RE BREAKING ISRAEL'S LAWS! YOU LET JEZEBEL BRING IN FALSE GODS—BUT JEHOVAH WILL DESTROY THEM!

AS THE LORD GOD OF ISRAEL LIVES, NO RAIN SHALL FALL ON YOUR LAND FOR YEARS!

THIS CRAZY PROPHET THREATENS US! SEIZE HIM, GUARDS!

BUT ELIJAH ESCAPED THE GUARDS---

AFTER HIM! HE'S GETTING AWAY!

NOW IN DANGER, HE WAS GUIDED TO GO TO THE BROOK CHERITH FOR REFUGE---

YOU WILL BE SAFE HERE--- DRINK OF THE BROOK- AND I HAVE COMMANDED THE RAVENS TO FEED YOU HERE!

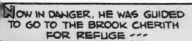

NEXT MORNING....

I AM VERY HUNGRY --BUT GOD HAS PROMISED TO SEND HIS RAVENS WITH FOOD FOR ME!

AS ELIJAH WATCHED---

BUT AFTER A TIME, AS ELIJAH HAD PROPHESIED, THE BROOK CHERITH DRIED UP IN THE DROUGHT THAT CAME UPON THE LAND---

I AM THIRSTY, BUT THE BROOK IS DRY- WHAT SHALL I DO NOW?

GO NOW TO THE TOWN OF ZAREPHATH- WHERE THERE IS A WIDOW WHO WILL HELP YOU!

AT THE GATE OF ZAREPHATH, ELIJAH SAW A WIDOW GATHERING STICKS FOR FIREWOOD---

THIS IS THE WOMAN WHO IS TO HELP ME!

BRING ME A MORSEL OF BREAD!

I HAVE NO BREAD, ONLY A LITTLE MEAL AND OIL --HARDLY ENOUGH TO KEEP ME AND MY SON ALIVE!

GO AND MAKE BREAD FROM THE MEAL AND OIL — THERE WILL BE ENOUGH FOR ALL OF US FOR MANY DAYS!

BY A MIRACLE, THE FEW HANDFULS OF MEAL AND THE FEW DROPS OF OIL DID BECOME MULTIPLIED MANY TIMES~~

THIS MORNING THERE WAS HARDLY A CUP LEFT!

HE MUST BE A HOLY MAN, MOTHER!

LATER, THE WOMAN'S SON GREW VERY ILL ~~~

I'M AFRAID! HE'S NOT BREATHING!

HAVE NO FEAR - GO AND LEAVE ME ALONE WITH HIM!

ELIJAH TAKES THE CHILD TO HIS OWN ROOM ~~~

GOD HAS HEARD MY PRAYER!

I'M WELL AGAIN!

SEE, YOUR SON IS HEALED!

BY THIS I KNOW THAT YOU ARE A MAN OF GOD, AND THAT THE WORD OF THE LORD IN YOUR MOUTH IS TRUTH!

MEANWHILE, NO RAIN FELL ON AHAB'S KINGDOM AND THE DROUGHT MADE EVERYONE SUFFER. AND GOD TOLD ELIJAH TO GO BACK AND SHOW HIMSELF TO AHAB. AS ELIJAH RETURNED, HE MET OBADIAH, SERVANT OF THE KING ~~~

CAN IT BE ELIJAH?

YES - GO AND TELL THE KING I AM HERE!

WILL YOU PROMISE TO BE HERE AND NOT DISAPPEAR AGAIN? IF YOU GO, KING AHAB WILL SLAY ME - HE'S LOOKING EVERYWHERE FOR YOU!

I PROMISE TO WAIT FOR HIM HERE!

So King Ahab goes to meet Elijah ~~

SO YOU'RE, THE MAN WHO MADE SO MUCH TROUBLE!

NOT I, BUT YOU, O KING, HAVE MADE TROUBLE! YOU HAVE TURNED TO WORSHIP BAAL, AND LED YOUR PEOPLE AWAY FROM GOD!

ELIJAH PROPOSED A TEST TO PROVE THAT BAAL WAS A FALSE GOD. HE ASKED THAT PRIESTS OF BAAL BE SUMMONED TO MOUNT CARMEL TO OFFER UP A BULLOCK TO BAAL ON ONE ALTAR, WHILE HE WOULD OFFER UP A BULLOCK ON THE ALTAR OF THE LORD ~~~~~~

WE'LL DO THAT - THEN THE GOD WHO ANSWERS US BY FIRE IS THE TRUE GOD!

IF ELIJAH'S GOD DOES THAT, THEN I'LL BELIEVE!

A TEST OF BAAL'S POWER!

22

And Elijah spoke to all the people ~~~

HOW LONG WILL YOU HALT BETWEEN TWO OPINIONS? IF THE LORD IS GOD, FOLLOW HIM - IF BAAL IS GOD, THEN FOLLOW HIM!

23

ON THE APPOINTED DAY, THE SACRIFICES WERE PLACED ON THE TWO ALTARS. FIRST THE 850 PRIESTS OF BAAL CALLED ON THEIR GOD ~~~

O BAAL, HEAR US!

PERHAPS YOUR GOD IS ASLEEP!

SPEAK TO US, O BAAL, WITH FIRE!

TO THE LORD GOD OF ISRAEL

TO BAAL THE SUN GOD

WHY DOESN'T HE ANSWER US?

24

So THEY CALLED UPON BAAL ALL DAY, BUT THERE WAS NO ANSWER ~~~

25

And at evening ~~~

COME NEAR TO ME, ALL YOU PEOPLE!

BAAL DIDN'T ANSWER!

WE'LL SEE WHETHER ELIJAH'S GOD WILL SPEAK!

26

FIRST ELIJAH COMMANDED THAT FOUR JARS OF WATER BE POURED ON THE OFFERING- ONCE, TWICE, THREE TIMES AND FOUR TIMES, TILL IT WAS DRENCHED ~~~

27

ELIJAH PRAYS TO THE LORD... O LORD, THE GOD OF ABRAHAM, OF ISAAC AND OF ISRAEL, LET IT BE KNOWN THIS DAY THAT YOU ARE GOD IN ISRAEL, AND THAT I AM YOUR SERVANT AND THAT I HAVE DONE ALL THESE THINGS ACCORDING TO YOUR WORD—HEAR ME, O LORD, HEAR ME, THAT THIS PEOPLE MAY KNOW THAT YOU, LORD, ART GOD!

AND AS ELIJAH PRAYED ---

THE LORD IS GOD!

ELIJAH'S GOD HAS SPOKEN—HE IS THE TRUE GOD!

LET US KILL THOSE LYING PRIESTS OF BAAL!

WHEN THE MEN SAW THAT BAAL WAS A FALSE GOD THEY DESTROYED THE FALSE PRIESTS AND THE DROUGHT WAS LIFTED ---

SOON GOD WILL SEND RAIN, AHAB!

PRAISE THE GOD OF ISRAEL!

LOOK! THERE'S A BLACK CLOUD ON THE HORIZON!

NOW OUR CATTLE WILL NOT DIE!

JEZEBEL WAS VERY ANGRY AT ELIJAH FOR PROVING HER GOD TO BE FALSE AND FOR KILLING HER PRIESTS ---

TELL ELIJAH HE'D BETTER GET OUT OF HERE, OR IT WILL NOT BE SAFE FOR HIM!

THE QUEEN WILL DO HIM HARM!

AT HER THREATS, ELIJAH AGAIN FLED FOR HIS LIFE, AND HID IN THE WILDERNESS ~~

I AM SO UNHAPPY, I WISH THE LORD WOULD TAKE AWAY MY LIFE!

ELIJAH HAD NO FOOD WITH HIM, AND THAT NIGHT HE WENT TO SLEEP HUNGRY — BUT AS HE SLEPT —

AWAKE, ELIJAH, AND EAT!

So much strength did this heavenly food give Elijah that he was able to travel forty days and forty nights to Mount Horeb, where the voice of God spoke to him ---

WHAT ARE YOU DOING HERE, ELIJAH?

THE CHILDREN OF ISRAEL SEEK MY LIFE BECAUSE I HAVE BEEN JEALOUS FOR THE LORD GOD OF HOSTS!

And the voice spoke again, and commanded Elijah to go to the mountain top ---

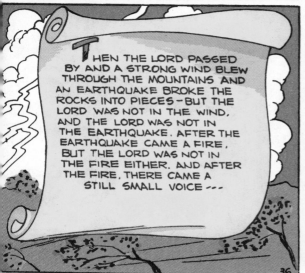

Then the Lord passed by and a strong wind blew through the mountains and an earthquake broke the rocks into pieces — but the Lord was not in the wind, and the Lord was not in the earthquake. After the earthquake came a fire, but the Lord was not in the fire either. And after the fire, there came a still small voice ---

And the voice spoke to Elijah ---

GO TO THE WILDERNESS OF DAMASCUS, AND ANOINT ONE TO BE KING OVER SYRIA — ANOINT JEHU TO BE KING OF ISRAEL AFTER WICKED AHAB RULES NO LONGER — AND ANOINT ELISHA, WHO WILL BE A GREAT PROPHET AFTER YOU!

Elijah finds the young farmer, Elisha, who is to carry on his work ---

THIS IS THE MAN!

Elijah cast his mantle on Elisha — a symbol that Elisha was to succeed him ---

YOU ARE TO FOLLOW ME AND DO MY WORK AFTER I AM GONE!

I'LL SERVE YOU, MASTER. JUST LET ME SAY GOODBYE TO MY FAMILY — I WILL COME AT ONCE!

STILL ISRAEL TOILED UNDER THE TYRANNY OF JEZEBEL, A STRONG QUEEN WITH A WEAK HUSBAND ---

YOU SHOULD NOT HAVE THEM WHIPPED SO, JEZEBEL!

WHAT KIND OF KING ARE YOU? IN MY COUNTRY WE WHIP DISOBEDIENT SLAVES!

ONE DAY KING AHAB WENT TO SEE FARMER NABOTH ---

THIS IS A BEAUTIFUL VINEYARD, NABOTH — SELL IT TO ME!

NO, SIRE — IT BELONGED TO MY FAMILY FOR YEARS — I WON'T SELL AT ANY PRICE!

AHAB RETURNED HOME ANGRY AND WOULDN'T EAT ANY DINNER ---

WHAT MAKES YOU SO SULLEN, AHAB?

I ASKED NABOTH TO SELL ME HIS VINEYARD AND HE REFUSED — UNDER THE LAW I CAN'T GET THE LAND!

AND YOU CALL YOURSELF A KING! COME ON, NOW, GET UP AND EAT YOUR DINNER — I'LL SEE THAT YOU GET THE VINEYARD!

WICKED JEZEBEL MAKES A PLOT AGAINST NABOTH ---

and have two men bear witness against Naboth, saying he blasphemed against God and the King

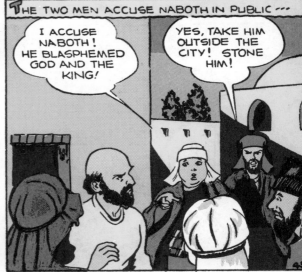

THE TWO MEN ACCUSE NABOTH IN PUBLIC ---

I ACCUSE NABOTH! HE BLASPHEMED GOD AND THE KING!

YES, TAKE HIM OUTSIDE THE CITY! STONE HIM!

NABOTH HAS BEEN STONED AND IS DEAD!

THERE NOW, AHAB! NABOTH IS DEAD— GO AND TAKE THE VINEYARD!

46

FOR UNDER THE LAW, WHEN A MAN DIED WITH NO HEIRS, HIS PROPERTY WENT TO THE KING ---

47

WHEN NEWS OF THIS TERRIBLE DEED REACHED ELIJAH, THE PROPHET WENT AT ONCE TO AHAB IN NABOTH'S STOLEN VINEYARD ---

YOU HAVE DONE EVIL! GOD WILL BE AVENGED— YOU AND JEZEBEL WILL DIE FOR SPILLING NABOTH'S BLOOD!

48

YEARS PASSED, AND THERE WAS WAR BETWEEN ISRAEL AND SYRIA. THE KING OF THE SYRIANS SOUGHT AHAB'S LIFE

MOST IMPORTANT OF ALL— FIND KING AHAB AND DESTROY HIM!

49

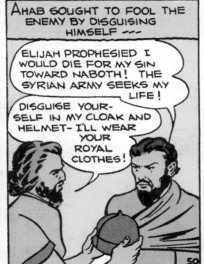

AHAB SOUGHT TO FOOL THE ENEMY BY DISGUISING HIMSELF ---

ELIJAH PROPHESIED I WOULD DIE FOR MY SIN TOWARD NABOTH! THE SYRIAN ARMY SEEKS MY LIFE!

DISGUISE YOURSELF IN MY CLOAK AND HELMET— I'LL WEAR YOUR ROYAL CLOTHES!

50

AT FIRST THE ENEMY PURSUED THE SOLDIER DRESSED IN AHAB'S GARMENTS ---

LOOK! THAT'S NOT KING AHAB!

YOU'RE RIGHT —IT'S NOT HIS FACE!

ANOTHER MAN IS DRESSED IN HIS CLOTHES— COME, LET'S SEEK THE REAL KING!

51

BUT WHILE THEY WERE SEARCHING ---

THE DISGUISE DIDN'T HELP — THE ENEMY'S ARROW HAS FOUND ME!

52

I'VE FOUGHT ALL DAY — NOW I DIE! AND ELIJAH'S PROPHECY IS FULFILLED!

53

WICKED QUEEN JEZEBEL STILL LIVED BUT PUNISHMENT WAS TO COME TO HER TOO, AS ELIJAH HAD ALSO PROPHESIED, FOR ALL THE SUFFERING SHE HAD CAUSED TO INNOCENT PEOPLE ---

54

The Story of ELISHA

FROM THE SECOND BOOK OF KINGS
(CHAPTERS 2-9)

WHEN ELIJAH'S EARTHLY WORK WAS DONE AND HE KNEW THAT GOD WAS ABOUT TO TAKE HIM UP TO HEAVEN, HE SET OUT FROM GILGAL WITH YOUNG ELISHA, WHO WAS TO TAKE OVER HIS WORK ~~~

GOD HAS COMMANDED ME TO GO TO THE RIVER JORDAN, ELISHA — BUT YOU DO NOT NEED TO COME!

AS THE LORD LIVES, MASTER, I WILL NOT LEAVE YOU!

WHEN THEY CAME TO THE RIVER JORDAN ELIJAH TOOK HIS MANTLE, ROLLED IT TOGETHER AND STRUCK THE WATERS. A MIRACLE HAPPENED — THE RIVER PARTED, AND THE TWO HOLY MEN PASSED OVER ON DRY GROUND ~~~

ELIJAH, BEFORE HE WAS TAKEN AWAY, OFFERED TO DO ONE LAST THING FOR ELISHA ~~~

I ONLY ASK YOU, ELIJAH, TO GIVE ME A DOUBLE PORTION OF YOUR SPIRIT!

YOU HAVE ASKED A HARD THING — NEVERTHELESS, IF YOU'RE ABLE TO SEE ME WHEN I AM TAKEN INTO HEAVEN, YOU SHALL BE GRANTED YOUR WISH!

A CHARIOT OF FIRE CAME IN A WHIRLWIND AND CARRIED ELIJAH AWAY. HE THREW HIS MANTLE TO ELISHA ~~~

MY FATHER, MY FATHER, I BEHOLD THE CHARIOT OF ISRAEL! MY PRAYER IS GRANTED! YOUR SPIRIT, ELIJAH, WILL NOW BE UPON ME!

ELISHA WITH ELIJAH'S MANTLE WENT TO JERICHO ~~~

THE SPIRIT OF ELIJAH RESTS ON ELISHA!

HE HAS THE POWER TO WORK MIRACLES!

THE CITY OF JERICHO GOT ITS WATER FROM A SPRING WHICH WAS BITTER, AND WHICH MADE THE GROUND BARREN ---

PURIFY THE WATER FOR US, ELISHA!

BRING ME SALT!

ELISHA CAST THE SALT INTO THE SPRING — AND THE WATERS BECAME SWEET AND PLEASANT FROM THAT DAY ---

GOD HEALS THESE WATERS!

WONDERFUL PURE WATER!

ELISHA IS TRULY A WORKER OF MIRACLES!

ELISHA WENT ALONE TO THE COUNTRY TO MEDITATE ---

GOD HAS BLESSED ME THUS FAR, BUT I MUST NOT FORGET THE TASK ELIJAH LEFT ME — TO CRUSH WICKED JEZEBEL, THE QUEEN!

THENCE, ELISHA WENT ON TO THE TOWN OF SHUNEM~

THERE GOES THE MAN OF GOD TO WHOM I GAVE BREAD THE OTHER DAY... HE PASSES BY OFTEN— LET US SUPPLY HIM WITH A ROOM AND A BED TO REST, A TABLE, STOOL AND CANDLESTICK!

AS YOU SAY, WIFE!

AND THAT LITTLE ROOM WILL BE YOURS, TO REST YOURSELF WHEN YOU COME HERE, HOLY MAN!

YOU ARE A KIND WOMAN!

I WILL PRAY TO GOD TO RESTORE LIFE TO THIS CHILD BECAUSE OF HIS MOTHER'S GOODNESS!

ELISHA WORKED A MIRACLE ~~~

HERE IS YOUR SON!

I'M WELL NOW, MOTHER!

I KNEW ELISHA COULD SAVE YOU!

IN GILGAL, THERE WAS A GREAT FAMINE WHEN ELISHA AND HIS SERVANT GEHAZI ARRIVED THERE ~~~

ELISHA, HELP US!

WE'RE STARVING!

WORK A MIRACLE AND GET FOOD FOR US!

MEANWHILE, MEN BROUGHT IN WILD GOURDS FROM THE FIELDS TO COOK FOR FOOD — BUT THE GOURDS WERE POISONOUS ~~~

O ELISHA, THERE IS DEATH IN THIS POT! THOUGH WE STARVE, WE CANNOT EAT THESE POISONOUS HERBS!

BRING ME A BOWL OF MEAL!

NOW IT IS NO LONGER POISONOUS! GIVE IT TO THE PEOPLE, THAT THEY MAY EAT!

A MIRACLE!

AND THE PEOPLE WERE FED! ELISHA HAD NEUTRALIZED THE POISON IN THE HERBS SO THAT THERE WAS NOT HARM BUT NOURISHMENT IN THEM! ~~~

26

LATER IN THE FAMINE A MAN CAME BRINGING TWENTY LOAVES OF BREAD FROM ANOTHER TOWN AS A GIFT TO ELISHA ~~~

GIVE IT TO THEM! FOR GOD HAS SAID, "THEY SHALL EAT AND THERE SHALL BE FOOD LEFT!"

WITH THIS LITTLE BIT OF FOOD, HOW AM I TO FEED A WHOLE CITY, ELISHA? BUT I OBEY!

27

AND SO IT PROVED—FOR BY A MIRACLE, THE SMALL BASKET OF BREAD WAS MORE THAN ENOUGH FOR THE HUNGRY PEOPLE OF GILGAL ~~~

NOW IN SYRIA LIVED A GREAT GENERAL, NAAMAN—A POWERFUL WARRIOR, BUT HE WAS AFFLICTED WITH LEPROSY ~~~

I'M IN DESPAIR! I CAN CONQUER ARMIES, BUT NOT THIS DISEASE OF LEPROSY!

IN MY HOME IN ISRAEL THERE IS A GREAT PROPHET, ELISHA... I KNOW HE CAN HEAL NAAMAN!

29

SO NAAMAN WENT TO THE LAND OF ISRAEL TO SEE ELISHA ~~~

ELISHA SAYS IF YOU WILL DIP SEVEN TIMES IN THE RIVER JORDAN, YOU SHALL BE HEALED!

WHAT KIND OF PROPHET IS THIS? I CAN WASH IN BETTER RIVERS IN DAMASCUS, MY HOMELAND!

30

BUT, GENERAL, TRY IT AT LEAST!

IF HE HAD TOLD YOU TO DO SOMETHING HARD, YOU'D HAVE DONE IT!

WHY NOT DO THIS EASY THING?

31

LATER...

FIVE TIMES I HAVE DIPPED AND I'M NOT HEALED!

ONLY TWICE MORE, NAAMAN!

32

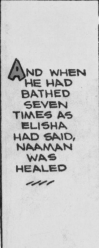

AND WHEN HE HAD BATHED SEVEN TIMES AS ELISHA HAD SAID, NAAMAN WAS HEALED ~

NOW I KNOW THERE IS NO GOD BUT THE GOD OF ISRAEL... LET ME MAKE A GIFT TO SHOW MY APPRECIATION!

I WANT NOTHING FOR MYSELF... I WAS ONLY USING GOD'S POWER TO HEAL YOU!

33

BUT GEHAZI, THE SERVANT OF ELISHA, THOUGHT THAT SOME REWARD SHOULD BE FORTHCOMING FROM NAAMAN FOR HIS HEALING ~~~

ELISHA LET NAAMAN OFF WITHOUT PAYING — WHY SHOULDN'T I GO AFTER HIM AND GET SOMETHING FOR MYSELF?

34

35

GEHAZI CHASES AFTER NAAMAN'S PARTY ~~~

WHAT IS IT, GEHAZI? WHY DO YOU COME AFTER ME?

ELISHA CHANGED HIS MIND — HE TOLD ME TO ASK YOU FOR SILVER AND GARMENTS!

36

GEHAZI GOES HOME, HIS MEN CARRYING THE GIFTS.

NAAMAN GAVE ME RICH PRESENTS! BUT I WON'T TELL ELISHA... WASN'T HE A FOOL! HE COULD HAVE HAD ALL THIS!

37

AT HOME AGAIN, GEHAZI HIDES THE GIFTS WITHOUT SAYING ANYTHING TO ELISHA — BUT, BEING A PROPHET, ELISHA KNOWS!

WHERE HAVE YOU BEEN, GEHAZI?

I-I-OH, I HAVEN'T BEEN ANYWHERE, ELISHA!

I WONDER HOW HE KNOWS?

38

DID YOU THINK I WOULD NOT KNOW, GEHAZI? IS THIS A TIME TO BE THINKING OF YOURSELF, OF GETTING MONEY AND OF EARTHLY THINGS? I HEALED NAAMAN THROUGH THE POWER OF GOD, AND YOU WANT TO PROFIT SELFISHLY BY IT!

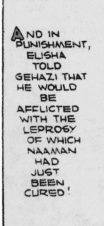

AND IN PUNISHMENT, ELISHA TOLD GEHAZI THAT HE WOULD BE AFFLICTED WITH THE LEPROSY OF WHICH NAAMAN HAD JUST BEEN CURED!

40

MEANWHILE, ELISHA HAD BEEN LAYING PLANS TO CRUSH WICKED JEZEBEL THROUGH PRINCE JEHU, A FINE AND NOBLE YOUNG PRINCE OF A NEIGHBORING TRIBE OF ISRAEL ---

GO TAKE THIS BOX, AND FIND PRINCE JEHU--ANOINT HIS HEAD WITH THIS OIL AND SAY, "GOD HAS APPOINTED YOU TO BE KING OF ISRAEL --YOUR MISSION --TO CRUSH JEZEBEL!"

I WILL DO AS YOU SAY, ELISHA!

41

ELISHA'S MESSENGER PROCLAIMED JEHU KING ---

AND I AM SENT TO ANOINT YOU KING OF ISRAEL - YOU SHALL DESTROY JEZEBEL!

I WILL GATHER ARMIES AND MARCH AGAINST HER AT ONCE!

42

MESSENGERS BROUGHT WORD TO JEZEBEL IN HER PALACE THAT A HOST WAS APPROACHING---

JEHU IS COMING WITH ARMIES! HE RIDES FURIOUSLY IN HIS CHARIOT OF WAR!

I AM NOT AFRAID OF JEHU!

43

VENGEANCE, JEZEBEL! YOUR TIME HAS COME! WHAT MEN ARE ON MY SIDE?

WE ARE WITH YOU, JEHU!

SHE HAS ABUSED US - WE'LL TURN HER OVER TO YOU!

44

LATER...

NOW JEZEBEL IS DEAD! SHE WILL DO NO MORE EVIL!

MY MISSION IS DONE! THROUGH YOU I HAVE DESTROYED FOREVER THE POWER OF THE WICKED QUEEN --- ISRAEL IS FREE!

45

I LEAVE YOU— RULE WISELY, JEHU! I HAVE FINISHED MY WORK-BUT IF EVER YOU NEED ME, I WILL RETURN!

YOU HAVE FREED ISRAEL FROM A WICKED WOMAN. I PROMISE TO RULE WISELY, TO OBEY YOU, AND TO FOLLOW GOD'S WILL!

SO ELISHA COMPLETED THE TASK GOD HAD GIVEN HIM, AND THE LAND OF ISRAEL WAS AT PEACE FOR MANY YEARS UNDER KING JEHU ---

46

The Story of ISAIAH
A GREAT PROPHET OF THE JEWS

FROM THE BOOK OF ISAIAH

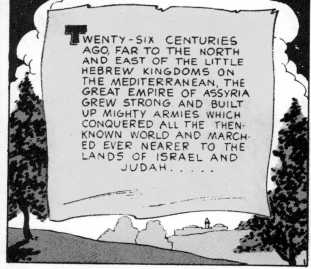

TWENTY-SIX CENTURIES AGO, FAR TO THE NORTH AND EAST OF THE LITTLE HEBREW KINGDOMS ON THE MEDITERRANEAN, THE GREAT EMPIRE OF ASSYRIA GREW STRONG, AND BUILT UP MIGHTY ARMIES WHICH CONQUERED ALL THE THEN-KNOWN WORLD AND MARCHED EVER NEARER TO THE LANDS OF ISRAEL AND JUDAH.....

WHEN OUR KING APPEASED THEM WITH SILVER, THEY TOOK IT—BUT THEIR ARMIES CAME BACK AGAIN!

MY SON ISAIAH — HE FEELS IT DEEPLY!

GOD PUNISHES US BECAUSE OUR PEOPLE ARE WICKED!

YOUNG ISAIAH, AFLAME WITH THE LOVE OF GOD AND OF HIS PEOPLE, SAW A WONDROUS VISION ONE DAY IN THE TEMPLE ...

HOLY, HOLY IS THE LORD OF HOSTS!

THE WHOLE EARTH IS FULL OF HIS GLORY!

WOE IS ME! FOR I AM UNDONE! MINE EYES HAVE SEEN THE KING, THE LORD OF HOSTS!

3

WHOM SHALL I SEND TO TELL MY PEOPLE?

HERE I AM — SEND ME!

4

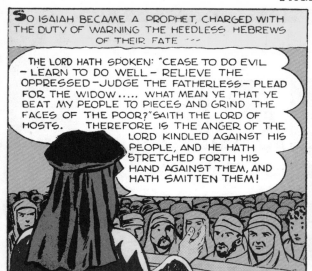

SO ISAIAH BECAME A PROPHET, CHARGED WITH THE DUTY OF WARNING THE HEEDLESS HEBREWS OF THEIR FATE ---

THE LORD HATH SPOKEN: "CEASE TO DO EVIL – LEARN TO DO WELL – RELIEVE THE OPPRESSED – JUDGE THE FATHERLESS – PLEAD FOR THE WIDOW ..... WHAT MEAN YE THAT YE BEAT MY PEOPLE TO PIECES AND GRIND THE FACES OF THE POOR?" SAITH THE LORD OF HOSTS. THEREFORE IS THE ANGER OF THE LORD KINDLED AGAINST HIS PEOPLE, AND HE HATH STRETCHED FORTH HIS HAND AGAINST THEM, AND HATH SMITTEN THEM!

BUT LIKE MANY ANOTHER PROPHET, ISAIAH WAS WITHOUT HONOR IN HIS OWN COUNTRY ---

DOOM IS APPROACHING – IF ONLY I COULD MAKE MY PEOPLE SEE!

I HAVE NO TIME!

WE'LL BE LATE TO THE FEAST!

MEANWHILE THE GREAT ASSYRIAN ARMIES UNDER TIGLATH-PILESER WERE ON THE MARCH, MOVING ALWAYS NEARER TO JERUSALEM ---

NOTHING WILL STOP US! WE'LL CONQUER THE WHOLE WORLD!

SOON WE'LL VANQUISH THE HEBREWS AND MAKE THEM OUR SLAVES!

ISAIAH CONTINUED TO TALK TO HIS PEOPLE ---

WOE UNTO THEM THAT CALL EVIL, GOOD; AND GOOD, EVIL! WOE UNTO THEM THAT ARE WISE IN THEIR OWN EYES! THEY HAVE CAST AWAY THE LAW OF THE LORD OF HOSTS! THEREFORE IS THE ANGER OF THE LORD KINDLED AGAINST HIS PEOPLE – HOWL YE! FOR THE DAY OF THE LORD IS AT HAND, AND HE WILL PUNISH THE WORLD FOR ITS EVIL!

MEANWHILE, TWO NEIGHBORING RULERS, KING PEKAH AND KING REZIN, SOUGHT TO MAKE A DEFENSE PACT AGAINST THE ASSYRIANS AND INVITED KING AHAZ OF JUDAH TO JOIN THEM ---

KING AHAZ REFUSES TO JOIN YOU!

WE'LL MARCH OUR ARMIES AGAINST JERUSALEM AND FORCE HIM TO JOIN US!

HE'S A COWARD!

ISAIAH MARRIED A PROPHETESS WHO BORE HIM TWO SONS. ONE DAY, AS ISAIAH WAS TEACHING HIS SONS IN THEIR LITTLE GARDEN ---

AND WHAT DOES MY NAME MEAN, FATHER?

YOUR NAME, SHEAR-JASHUB, MEANS "A REMNANT SHALL RETURN UNTO GOD AND BE SAVED."

HASTEN, ISAIAH! NEWS! JERUSALEM IS BESIEGED!

ISAIAH'S HEART WAS MOVED AT THIS NEWS, AS TREES ARE MOVED WITH THE WIND... AND GOD SPOKE AND COMMANDED HIM TO GO WITH HIS YOUNG SON SHEAR-JASHUB AND TALK WITH KING AHAZ ---

THEY MET BESIDE THE UPPER POOL, THE KING, THE PROPHET AND THE CHILD ---

WHAT WILL BECOME OF US?

HAVE NO FEAR! THE LORD COMMANDS YOU NOT TO BE FAINT-HEARTED. THE ARMIES SHALL NOT TAKE JERUSALEM. LET POWERFUL NATIONS FIGHT IF THEY WILL — THERE IS ONLY ONE WAY IN WHICH WE CAN BE STRONG — BY PLACING OUR FAITH IN GOD!

CAN I TRUST IN GOD ALONE? IS IT NOT BETTER TO MAKE FRIENDS WITH SO STRONG AN ENEMY AS THE ASSYRIANS?

NO! GOD WILL SAVE US! THE KINGS WHO THREATEN YOU WILL BE DESTROYED AND THEIR LANDS WILL BE LAID WASTE... BUT YOU MUST HAVE FAITH. OTHERWISE YOU, TOO, WILL SHARE THEIR FATE!

DESPITE AHAZ AND HIS WEAK WILL, THE THREAT TO JERUSALEM WAS WITHDRAWN THAT TIME AND THE CITY WAS SAFE.....
FINALLY AHAZ, WHO HAD BEEN A WICKED KING, DIED, AND HEZEKIAH, HIS SON — A GOOD MAN — BECAME THE RULER. OVER HEZEKIAH, TOO, HUNG THE SHADOW OF THE POWERFUL NATION ASSYRIA, WITH ITS HUGE AND GREEDY ARMIES, NOW LED BY A NEW KING — SENNACHERIB.

...AS THE ENEMY DREW NEAR TO JERUSALEM ---

I HAVE NEWS, KING HEZEKIAH! THE ASSYRIANS HAVE CAPTURED THE CITY OF DAMASCUS!

WE ARE IN THEIR PATH! WE'LL BE NEXT!

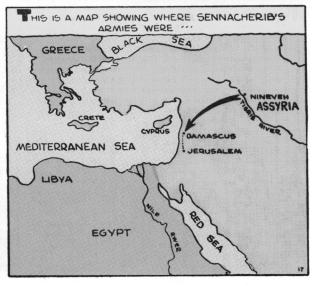

THIS IS A MAP SHOWING WHERE SENNACHERIB'S ARMIES WERE ---

GREECE
BLACK SEA
CRETE
CYPRUS
MEDITERRANEAN SEA
NINEVEH
ASSYRIA
TIGRIS RIVER
DAMASCUS
JERUSALEM
LIBYA
NILE RIVER
EGYPT
RED SEA

WE MUST HAVE HELP! I WILL MAKE AN ALLIANCE WITH THE EGYPTIANS!

WOE TO THEM THAT TRUST IN CHARIOTS AND HORSEMEN, BUT LOOK NOT TO THE LORD. GOD WILL PROTECT JERUSALEM. HAS HE NOT TOLD US, IN QUIETNESS AND IN CONFIDENCE SHALL BE YOUR STRENGTH?

THE ASSYRIAN ARMIES CAMP ON THE PLAINS BEFORE JERUSALEM ~~

KING HEZEKIAH OFFERS TO PAY HEAVY TRIBUTE OF GOLD IF YOU WILL WITHDRAW YOUR ARMIES, KING SENNACHERIB!

WE'LL TAKE ALL HIS TREASURE!

IN JERUSALEM, THE PEOPLE COLLECT GOLD ~~

I WOULD RATHER DIE THAN DO THIS!

THE ASSYRIANS WILL KILL US IF WE DO NOT GIVE THEM ALL OUR GOLD, EVEN THE GOLDEN ORNAMENTS OF OUR HOLY TEMPLE!

EVEN THESE RICH GIFTS DID NOT SATISFY THE ASSYRIANS ~~

WHAT OF YOUR GOLD? THAT WON'T STOP US! NOR WILL YOUR GOD! NO GOD HAS BEEN ABLE TO HALT THE ASSYRIAN ARMIES!

WICKED ONES!

WE'LL STARVE!

THEY WILL BESIEGE US!

IN THIS DARK HOUR, HEZEKIAH PRAYED IN THE TEMPLE ~~

O LORD OUR GOD, SAVE US FROM THEIR HANDS, THAT ALL THE KINGDOMS OF THE EARTH MAY KNOW THAT THOU ART THE LORD, EVEN THOU ONLY!

RETURNED TO THE PALACE, HEZEKIAH RECEIVES A MESSAGE FROM ISAIAH ~~

"THEREFORE THUS SAITH THE LORD CONCERNING THE KING OF ASSYRIA: HE SHALL NOT COME INTO THIS CITY, NOR SHOOT AN ARROW THERE! FOR I WILL DEFEND THIS CITY TO SAVE IT, FOR MY OWN SAKE."

And that night, in the camp of the Assyrians ...

THIS ILLNESS CAME UPON ME QUICKLY!

I'D HELP YOU - BUT I TOO AM SICK!

THE WHOLE CAMP IS STRICKEN WITH THIS STRANGE AILMENT!

24

And by morning, one hundred and twenty-five thousand of the enemies of Jerusalem had been struck down with the mysterious plague — and Sennacherib fled back to Assyria with the men who were left alive!

25

A year later ---

JUST ONE YEAR TODAY, OH KING, SINCE GOD DELIVERED US!

NEWS COMES THAT EVEN SENNACHERIB IS NOW DEAD — KILLED BY HIS TWO JEALOUS SONS IN THE CITY OF NINEVEH!

26

YOU WOULD NOT BELIEVE ME, OH KING, WHEN I TOLD YOU WHAT THE LORD GOD WOULD DO!

THE LIVING SHALL PRAISE HIM, AS I DO THIS DAY — AND THE FATHER SHALL MAKE KNOWN THE TRUTH TO HIS CHILDREN!

27

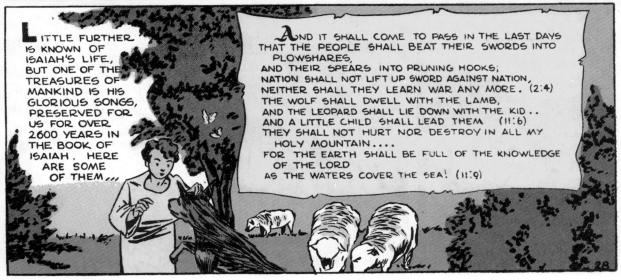

Little further is known of Isaiah's life, but one of the treasures of mankind is his glorious songs, preserved for us for over 2600 years in the book of Isaiah. Here are some of them ....

And it shall come to pass in the last days that the people shall beat their swords into plowshares,
And their spears into pruning hooks;
Nation shall not lift up sword against nation,
Neither shall they learn war any more. (2:4)
The wolf shall dwell with the lamb,
And the leopard shall lie down with the kid ..
And a little child shall lead them (11:6)
They shall not hurt nor destroy in all my holy mountain....
For the earth shall be full of the knowledge of the Lord
As the waters cover the sea! (11:9)

28

The Story of
JOSIAH
THE YOUNG KING OF THE JEWS
FROM 2ND KINGS, CHAPTERS 22 AND 23 AND 2ND CHRONICLES, CHAPTERS 34 THROUGH 36

JOSIAH WAS A BOY OF EIGHT YEARS WHEN HE BECAME THE 17TH KING OF THE JEWISH NATION CALLED JUDAH ---

MY SON, YOU ARE CALLED TO RULE IN TROUBLESOME TIMES!

FOLLOW YOUR MOTHER'S ADVICE AND KEEP CLOSE TO GOD, AND YOU WILL BE A GOOD AND WISE KING!

AS MY ANCESTORS SOUGHT WISDOM, SO MUST I!

DO THAT WHICH IS RIGHT AND RULE AS KING DAVID RULED BEFORE YOU!

IDOLATRY HAD TAKEN HOLD OF THE PEOPLE EVEN AMONG MEN OF RANK AND INFLUENCE ---

IDOLATRY HAS BECOME A NATIONAL EVIL - LET US GET RID OF IT!

UNDER JOSIAH'S DECREE AND PERSONAL SUPERVISION, IDOLS, IDOL TEMPLES AND ALTARS WERE DESTROYED ---

LET US MAKE A COMPLETE JOB OF IT, SO OUR PEOPLE WILL RETURN TO WORSHIP OF OUR TRUE GOD!

TOO LONG HAVE WE BEEN MISLED!

WHEN THE LAND HAD BEEN PURIFIED FROM IDOLATRY, JOSIAH, NOW A YOUNG MAN OF 26, DECIDED TO REPAIR AND BEAUTIFY THE TEMPLE, LONG NEGLECTED ---

GO, FAITHFUL SHAPHAN, TO HILKIAH, THE HIGH PRIEST. GIVE HIM THE TEMPLE MONEY AND HAVE HIM GET WORKMEN TO REPAIR THE HOUSE OF GOD!

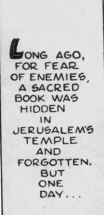

LONG AGO, FOR FEAR OF ENEMIES, A SACRED BOOK WAS HIDDEN IN JERUSALEM'S TEMPLE AND FORGOTTEN. BUT ONE DAY...

THIS WAS FOUND IN THE WALLS!

WE CANNOT READ, BUT YOU, HILKIAH, OUR HIGH PRIEST, CAN!

LET ME SEE IT!

THIS IS THE BOOK OF DEUTERONOMY, LONG LOST! I WILL HAVE SHAPHAN TAKE IT TO KING JOSIAH!

HILKIAH, WHAT IS IT? I'M ON MY WAY TO THE KING NOW!

I MUST READ THIS FIRST — IT IS ASTONISHING! THE OLD LAWS OF ISRAEL FOUND! JOSIAH WILL BE SURPRISED — THE KINGDOM'S LAWS HAVE BEEN MISCONSTRUED!

SO SHAPHAN WENT BEFORE JOSIAH ---

THESE ARE THE AUTHENTIC LAWS OF MOSES, SIRE!

HOW DISGRACEFULLY WE HAVE NEGLECTED THIS BOOK! I'LL DO SOMETHING ABOUT IT IMMEDIATELY!

I WILL PRESENT THIS GREAT DISCOVERY TO OUR PEOPLE — BUT FIRST WE MUST PRAY AND ASK GOD'S GUIDANCE!

I SHALL CALL THE CHIEF MEN AND PRIESTS TOGETHER, AND WITH GOD'S GUIDANCE WE WILL KNOW WHAT TO DO!

THE PRIESTS DECIDE TO CONSULT A HOLY AND INSPIRED WOMAN NAMED HULDAH

IF WHAT YOU SAY IS TRUE, THE REAL LAWS MUST BE PROCLAIMED TO THE PEOPLE AND OBEYED! TELL KING JOSIAH THAT THE JUDGMENTS AGAINST THE DISOBEDIENT WILL NOT FALL UPON HIM. HE IS TRYING TO SERVE GOD FAITHFULLY!

TO MAKE THE EVENT IMPRESSIVE, JOSIAH DECIDED TO RENEW THE CELEBRATION OF THE PASSOVER FEAST, A CUSTOM LONG NEGLECTED ---

SEND WORD TO ALL THE PEOPLE IN JUDEA AND ISRAEL TO COME TOGETHER IN THE RESTORED TEMPLE TO HEAR THE WORD OF GOD!

AN EIGHT-DAY CELEBRATION WAS HELD WITH SINGING AND FESTIVITY BY MORE THAN 30,000 PEOPLE, DURING WHICH TIME JOSIAH READ FROM THE LOST BOOK ---

THESE COMMANDMENTS ARE THE SACRED WORDS OF MOSES. LET US PROMISE TO OBEY THEM!

GOD GRANT WE NEVER NEGLECT THE BOOK AGAIN!

THE CELEBRATION INCLUDED GREAT FEASTS FROM THE KING'S ROYAL BOUNTY OF SUPPLIES ---

THIS IS THE HAPPIEST DAY OF MY LIFE. THE LAWS OF GOD HAVE NOW BEEN PUT TO WORK. OUR NATION IS BEING UNITED AS IN THE DAYS OF DAVID!

FOLLOWING THE ENTHUSIASM OF THE PASSOVER CELEBRATION, THE LAST REMNANTS OF IDOLATRY WERE WIPED OUT BY THE DESTRUCTION OF THE IDOLS, THE ALTARS AND THE IDOLATROUS PRIESTS ---

BUT TIMES WERE BAD — EGYPT THREATENED ---

THE POWER OF EGYPT IS COMING! A VAST ARMY!

WE'LL GO TO MEET THEM!

JOSIAH, CALLING THE ARMY, TAKES THE LEAD.

FOLLOW! WE SHALL FIGHT UNDER GOD!

FOR JOSIAH AND ISRAEL!

ON!

20

ON THE PLAIN OF ESDRAELON ---

WE'LL HOLD THEM HERE IN MEGIDDO!

THE EGYPTIANS ATTACK!

21

THE EGYPTIANS BREAK INTO THE FORT ---

HOLD! THE KING IS STRUCK!

WE ARE OUTNUMBERED!

22

AFTER JOSIAH'S DEATH AND ISRAEL'S DEFEAT, JOSIAH'S SON, JEHOAHAZ, TOOK HIS PLACE ON THE THRONE.

23

MY FATHER, JOSIAH, REIGNED AS A GOOD KING FOR 31 YEARS. I SHALL CONTINUE TO ENFORCE THE LAWS OF GOD FROM THE SACRED BOOK JOSIAH FOUND. RIGHT SHALL RULE!

HAIL! WE SHALL SURVIVE BY WORSHIPPING THE TRUE GOD!

24

BUT AFTER THREE MONTHS JEHOAHAZ WAS IMPRISONED BY PHARAOH -- NECHOH, AND ELIAKIM, ANOTHER SON OF JOSIAH, WAS PLACED UPON THE THRONE AND RENAMED JEHOIAKIM.

25

The Story of ESTHER
QUEEN OF PERSIA

FROM INDIA TO ETHIOPIA REIGNED A KING, WHOSE NAME WAS AHASUERUS. HE ORDERED MESSENGERS TO BE SENT THROUGHOUT THE LAND TO SEEK A FAIR MAIDEN TO BE CHOSEN FOR HIS QUEEN~~

ARRANGED FROM THE BOOK OF ESTHER

THE MESSENGERS, KING AHASUERUS, HAVE BEEN SENT!

THE UNMARRIED MAIDENS WILL BE CARED FOR HERE UNTIL I CHOOSE ONE TO BE MY QUEEN OF PERSIA!

HEGE, KEEPER OF THE WOMEN, WATCHES OVER THOSE WHO FLOCK TO THE COURT AT SHUSHAN~

ALL WILL HAVE CARE AND A HEARING, SO BE PATIENT!

NOW AMONG THEM WAS ESTHER, WARD OF MORDECAI, THE ISRAELITE~~

MORDECAI SAID MY BEAUTY WOULD WIN THE KING! - I MUST BE NICE TO HEGE, THE CHAMBERLAIN!

I AM PLEASED WITH YOU, MAIDEN! - BUT BE PATIENT!

I MUST NOT SAY I'M AN ISRAELITE YET!

MORDECAI KEPT WATCH DAILY ~~~

I'LL WATCH AND WAIT FOR NEWS EACH DAY— ESTHER WILL GET MESSAGES TO ME!

IN THE 7TH YEAR OF THE KING'S REIGN, ESTHER COMES BEFORE AHASUERUS

YOU PLEASE ME— COME, STAND UP!

So ESTHER IS CHOSEN QUEEN ABOVE ALL ~~~

YOU ARE NOW MY QUEEN, ESTHER!

I SHALL BE FAITHFUL, SIRE!

A FESTIVAL IS HELD ~~~

THIS FETE, IN CELEBRATION OF THE QUEEN, IS SPLENDID!

ESTHER WILL MAKE A WONDERFUL QUEEN!

SHE IS SO BEAUTIFUL!

EARLY EACH MORNING, MORDECAI IS AT THE KING'S GATE. HE OVERHEARS A PLOT~

ALL IS READY TO SEIZE THE KING, TERESH?

YES, BIGTHAN! - WE'LL LAY HANDS ON AHASUERUS!

MORDECAI DASHES TO GIVE WARNING ~

THE KING'S LIFE IS IN DANGER. I'LL GET WORD TO ESTHER! SHE'LL TELL HIM!!

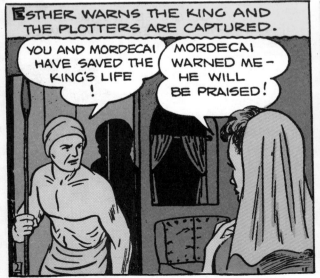

ESTHER WARNS THE KING AND THE PLOTTERS ARE CAPTURED.

YOU AND MORDECAI HAVE SAVED THE KING'S LIFE !

MORDECAI WARNED ME - HE WILL BE PRAISED!

So IT WAS WRITTEN IN THE RECORDS THAT MORDECAI SAVED THE KING'S LIFE ~

...BUT MORDECAI DISCOVERED THE PLOT AND THE MEN WERE HANGED !

THE KING HAD PROMOTED ONE OF HIS PRINCES, HAMAN, AND ORDERED ALL THE PEOPLE TO BOW BEFORE HIM~~

WHO ARE YOU? WHY DO YOU NOT BOW?

I AM MORDECAI. I BOW ONLY TO MY GOD!

THAT ISRAELITE, MORDECAI, DID NOT BOW, HAMAN!

I AM WRATHFUL! HE SHALL BE MADE TO HONOR ME!!

HAMAN GOES TO THE KING WITH AN EVIL SCHEME~~

CERTAIN PEOPLE DO NOT KEEP YOUR LAWS NOR SHOW RESPECT, SIRE—LET THEM BE DESTROYED!

DO WITH THEM AS SEEMS GOOD TO YOU!

I SHALL MAKE THE DECREE TO DESTROY, TO KILL, TO CAUSE TO PERISH, ALL JEWS IN ONE DAY—THE 13TH DAY OF ADAR, THE 12TH MONTH—AND TAKE THEIR PROPERTY!

MORDECAI SENDS WORD TO ESTHER THAT SHE MUST APPEAL TO THE KING TO SAVE THE LIVES OF HER PEOPLE~

BUT NO ONE CAN SEE THE KING UPON PAIN OF DEATH UNLESS THE KING ASKS HIM TO ENTER!!

TO THIS MORDECAI SENDS WORD— "IF YOUR PEOPLE PERISH, YOU WILL PERISH. YOU MUST SAVE US!"

I'LL DO IT! LET MORDECAI AND THE JEWS FAST AND PRAY. THEN I'LL GO TO THE KING, IF I HAVE TO DIE FOR IT!

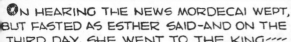

ON HEARING THE NEWS MORDECAI WEPT, BUT FASTED AS ESTHER SAID—AND ON THE THIRD DAY, SHE WENT TO THE KING——

WELCOME — WHAT IS YOUR REQUEST? IT SHALL BE GRANTED!

SO BE IT!

LET PRINCE HAMAN COME TO A BANQUET I HAVE PREPARED— HE WITH YOU!

LATER

I MUST STUDY HAMAN NOW!

I AM HONORED!

WHAT IS YOUR PETITION? IT SHALL BE GRANTED, AS I'VE PROMISED!

COME TOMORROW TO DINNER, AND I SHALL HAVE A REQUEST—BOTH YOU AND HAMAN COME!

HAMAN, BELIEVING HIMSELF IN ESTHER'S FAVOR, TELLS HIS WIFE AND FRIENDS——

ONLY ONE THING— MORDECAI, THE JEW, WILL NOT BOW TO ME!

THEN BUILD A GALLOWS —HANG HIM!

GOOD IDEA!

IT SHALL BE DONE AT ONCE! A GALLOWS FIFTY CUBITS HIGH! — MORDECAI SHALL HANG THERE!!

ONE NIGHT, THE KING IS LOOKING OVER THE RECORDS——

HAVE ANY HONORS BEEN GIVEN MORDECAI, WHO UNCOVERED THE PLOT ON MY LIFE?

NONE, SIRE!

ANY BUSINESS, SIRE?

WHAT SHALL BE DONE TO A MAN WHOM THE KING WISHES TO HONOR?

HE MEANS ME, OF COURSE!

LET THE KING GIVE HIM ROYAL CLOTHES, A HORSE, AND MARCH HIM THROUGH THE STREETS IN YOUR HONOR!!

THEN DO SO WITH MORDECAI, WHO SAVED ME!

MORDECAI IS LED THROUGH THE STREETS IN THE KING'S GARMENTS—LED BY THE ENVIOUS HAMAN———

HAIL MORDECAI, WHO SAVED AHASUERUS!

HAIL THE HERO!

AT HOME AGAIN, HAMAN TALKS TO HIS WIFE AND FRIENDS

I AM READY TO GO TO ESTHER'S BANQUET— I AM FAVORED! ONLY THIS MORDECAI BOTHERS ME!!

I, ZERESH, SAY HE SHALL YET HANG ON YOUR GALLOWS!

[5]

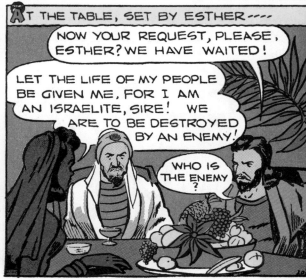

AT THE TABLE, SET BY ESTHER———

NOW YOUR REQUEST, PLEASE, ESTHER? WE HAVE WAITED!

LET THE LIFE OF MY PEOPLE BE GIVEN ME, FOR I AM AN ISRAELITE, SIRE! WE ARE TO BE DESTROYED BY AN ENEMY!

WHO IS THE ENEMY?

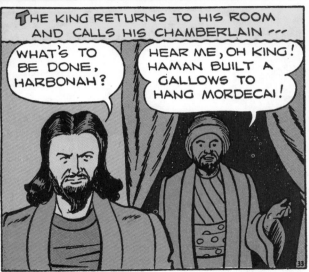

THE END

The Story of The Prophet JEREMIAH

FROM THE BOOK OF JEREMIAH

IN THE VILLAGE OF ANATHOTH, NOT FAR FROM THE GREAT CITY OF JERUSALEM, THE BOY JEREMIAH GREW UP ///

IN HIS EARLY YEARS, JEREMIAH KNEW THAT HE HAD A LIFE WORK TO PERFORM ///

WHATSOEVER I COMMAND, YOU SHALL SAY—DO NOT BE AFRAID, FOR I AM WITH YOU!

NOW AT THAT TIME THE KINGDOM OF JUDAH WAS IN THE MIDST OF TROUBLED DAYS. HER PEOPLE, WEAKENED BY EVIL, WERE BE-SET FROM WITHOUT BY THE ARMIES OF SCYTHIAN CONQUERORS ///

STOP THIS CAROUSING! THE CITY WILL BE LOST! THE SCYTHIAN ARMIES ARE MARCHING AGAINST US!

THAT TIME, THE SCYTHIANS WERE BEATEN BACK. BUT STILL THE PEOPLE OF JUDAH LIVED WICKED LIVES, OPPRESSING THE POOR, MURDERING, AND BREAKING THE COMMANDMENTS ///

GOD COMMANDED JEREMIAH TO LIFT HIS VOICE AGAINST THESE WRONGS ///

HEAR THE WORD OF THE LORD! DO NO WRONG, DO NO VIOLENCE TO THE STRANGER, THE FATHERLESS OR THE WIDOW, NOR SHED INNOCENT BLOOD!

IF YOU DO, FOREIGN ARMIES SHALL ENTER IN AT OUR GATES AND SIT ON THE THRONE OF OUR KING, AND THE LAND OF JUDAH WILL BE DESOLATE!

THE KING HAS FORBIDDEN ME TO PREACH, BUT GOD'S MESSAGE MUST REACH MY PEOPLE IN SOME WAY—THEREFORE, BARUCH, SINCE YOU CAN WRITE, PUT DOWN THESE WORDS ON THIS SHEEPSKIN PARCHMENT—

BUT KING JEHOIAKIM SEIZED THE WRITINGS AND BURNED THEM ～～～

CRAZY PROPHET! I'LL BURN WHAT HE WRITES!

GOD THEN COMMANDED JEREMIAH TO TAKE ANOTHER PARCHMENT AND TO LET BARUCH WRITE AGAIN ALL THE WORDS WHICH WERE IN THE FIRST PARCHMENT ～～～

AND JEREMIAH'S PROPHECY CAME TRUE AS THE ARMIES OF NEBUCHADNEZZAR, KING OF BABYLON, BESIEGED JERUSALEM ～～

THE BABYLONIANS FINALLY CONQUERED, AND THE PEOPLE OF JUDAH WERE CARRIED OFF TO CAPTIVITY ～～～

WHILE NEBUCHADNEZZAR PLACED ON THE THRONE A KING NAMED ZEDEKIAH WHO WOULD DO HIS BIDDING ～～～

NEBUCHADNEZZAR ORDERS THAT WE CROWN YOU KING!

DO AS WE TELL YOU AND YOU'LL PROSPER!

I'LL DO YOUR BIDDING, MASTERS!

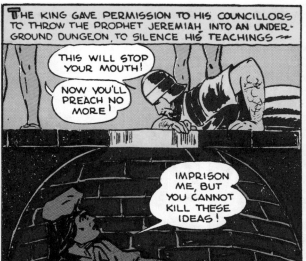

THE KING GAVE PERMISSION TO HIS COUNCILLORS TO THROW THE PROPHET JEREMIAH INTO AN UNDERGROUND DUNGEON, TO SILENCE HIS TEACHINGS —

THIS WILL STOP YOUR MOUTH!

NOW YOU'LL PREACH NO MORE!

IMPRISON ME, BUT YOU CANNOT KILL THESE IDEAS!

MEANWHILE, IN THE PALACE OF KING ZEDEKIAH, EBED-MELECH, THE ETHIOPIAN, SPEAKS UP FOR JEREMIAH —

YOUR COUNCILLORS HAVE DONE A WICKED THING TO JEREMIAH, OH KING! HE WILL DIE IN THAT PRISON CELL!

GO AND FREE HIM THEN!

YOU ARE A GOOD MAN, EBBED-MELECH!

BECAUSE I REVERE YOUR GOODNESS, JEREMIAH!

A FEW YEARS LATER ZEDEKIAH, INFLUENCED BY THE RULERS OF EGYPT, REBELLED AGAINST NEBUCHADNEZZAR, AND BROUGHT DOWN ON THE CITY ONCE MORE THE ARMIES OF BABYLON —

THIS TIME WE'LL TEAR JERUSALEM DOWN!

WE'LL HUMBLE ZEDEKIAH FOR DARING TO REVOLT!

THE SIEGE OF JERUSALEM (588 B.C.) WAS ONE OF THE MOST HORRIBLE IN BIBLICAL HISTORY. IT LASTED A YEAR AND A HALF. FIRE, SWORD AND FAMINE MADE TERRIBLE SUFFERING FOR THE PEOPLE —

IN THE BLACKEST MOMENT, ZEDEKIAH REMEMBERED THE WISE PROPHET JEREMIAH AND SENT FOR HIM —

JEREMIAH, I WOULD ASK YOU ONE THING —HIDE NOTHING FROM ME!

YOU CAN'T WIN — SURRENDER! YOU WILL SAVE YOUR LIFE AND YOUR CITY!

I AM AFRAID!

SO ZEDEKIAH STUBBORNLY WENT ON RESISTING. THE BABYLONIANS BROKE THROUGH THE WALLS OF JERUSALEM AND ENTERED THE CITY —

ZEDEKIAH WITH HIS HOUSEHOLD FLED TO THE PLAINS OF JERICHO, BUT HE WAS OVERTAKEN.

SURRENDER, KING ZEDEKIAH, IN THE NAME OF NEBUCHADNEZZAR!

ZEDEKIAH WAS BLINDED AND TAKEN TO BABYLON AS A CAPTIVE, WHILE SOLDIERS OF NEBUCHADNEZZAR BURNED THE CITY OF JERUSALEM AND TORE DOWN ITS WALLS —

MEANWHILE, INSIDE RAVAGED JERUSALEM —

JEREMIAH WAS RIGHT! HE PROPHESIED THIS, BUT WE WOULDN'T LISTEN!

ALL THIS TIME JEREMIAH HAD BEEN LIVING WITHIN THE PRISON, THOUGH NOT AS A PRISONER. NOW, HOWEVER —

THAT SHOULD BE JEREMIAH!

WE HAVE ORDERS TO TAKE YOU WITH US!

HE TOLD THE JUDEANS TO SURRENDER — WE WON'T HARM HIM!

IF YOU WISH TO GO TO BABYLON, WE WILL PROVIDE FOR YOU — BUT IF NOT, GO WHERE YOU WANT TO GO. YOU ARE FREE NOW!

I WILL STAY HERE WITH MY PEOPLE, WITH GEDALIAH WHOM THE KING OF BABYLON HAS MADE GOVERNOR OVER THE CITIES OF JUDAH.

SO JEREMIAH DWELT WITH GEDALIAH, AND THE JEWS WHO HAD BEEN DRIVEN FROM THEIR COUNTRY CAME BACK, AND HARVESTED THE SUMMER FRUITS —

FOR THE PRESENT, ALL SEEMS PEACE — IF NO MORE TROUBLE IS BREWING!

BUT TROUBLE SOON COMMENCED FOR GEDALIAH WAS SLAIN BY A MAN WHO DISTRUSTED HIM---

HELP! I'VE BEEN STABBED!

NOW, MORE TROUBLE!

WHAT WILL BABYLON DO ABOUT THIS?

WE'LL BE MADE TO SUFFER!

LET'S GO INTO THE LAND OF EGYPT, WHERE WE SHALL SEE NO WAR, NOR HEAR THE SOUND OF THE TRUMPETS NOR BE HUNGRY FOR BREAD-- AND THERE WILL WE DWELL!

LET'S ASK JEREMIAH WHAT HE THINKS!

AND THE LORD GOD SAYS, YOU MUST NOT GO INTO EGYPT, BUT REMAIN HERE IN YOUR OWN LAND. DO NOT BE AFRAID, HE SAYS, FOR I AM WITH YOU, AND WILL SAVE YOU. IF ANY GO INTO EGYPT, DOOM WILL OVERTAKE THEM THERE ANYWAY!

NEVERTHELESS, THIS LITTLE REMNANT OF THE JEWISH PEOPLE WENT INTO EGYPT, DISOBEYING THE WORD OF THE LORD, AND THEY TOOK JEREMIAH WITH THEM, AGAINST HIS WILL ---

IT ISN'T SAFE TO STAY! THE BABYLONIANS WILL KILL US!

WE LEAVE TONIGHT FOR EGYPT, AND YOU'LL COME WITH US!

THAT WILL NOT SAVE YOU -- YOU'LL FIND PEACE ONLY THROUGH GOD!

A FEW DAYS JOURNEY NOW, AND WE'RE OUT OF DANGER!

NO! THERE'S NO ESCAPE IN FLIGHT! YOU CAN'T RUN AWAY FROM THINGS!

EGYPT IS NOT FAR OFF NOW --THEN FREEDOM FROM OUR TROUBLES!

JEREMIAH GAVE US WRONG ADVICE, TELLING US TO STAY!

NO-FOR YOU WON'T BE FREE WHILE YOU'RE CHAINED TO YOUR WICKEDNESS!

DO YOU NOT REMEMBER ALL THE WRONG THINGS YOU DID, WORSHIPPING FALSE GODS, BREAKING THE COMMANDMENTS? BECAUSE THE LORD COULD NO LONGER BEAR ALL THIS, OUR LAND IS DESOLATE AND ACCURSED TODAY, AND WITHOUT AN INHABITANT!

FINALLY THE LITTLE BAND CAME TO EGYPT AND LIVED THERE ...

HERE AT LAST!

BUT WILL WE EVER RETURN TO OUR OWN LAND AGAIN?

JEREMIAH CONTINUED TO PREACH TO HIS PEOPLE EVEN IN THE DARKNESS AND SORROW OF EXILE

"GOD SAYS 'BUT FEAR NOT, AND BE NOT DISMAYED, OH ISRAEL' FOR BEHOLD, I WILL SAVE YOU FROM AFAR OFF... FEAR NOT, FOR I AM WITH THEE... FOR I WILL MAKE A FULL END OF ALL THE NATIONS WHITHER I HAVE DRIVEN YOU - BUT I WILL CORRECT YOU IN MEASURE

"DECLARE YE AMONG THE NATIONS..... BABYLON IS TAKEN! FOR OUT OF THE NORTH THERE COMES A NATION AGAINST HER WHICH SHALL MAKE HER LAND DESOLATE, AND NONE SHALL DWELL THEREIN!"

FAR FROM HIS HOMELAND OF JUDAH, JEREMIAH GREW OLD AND DIED ...

PERHAPS IF WE HAD LISTENED TO HIM!

HE WAS THE GREATEST AMONG US!

BUT LONG AFTER HIS DEATH, JEREMIAH'S PROPHECY DID COME TRUE, AND THE GREAT EMPIRE OF BABYLON, OPPRESSOR OF HIS PEOPLE, CRUMBLED BEFORE THE ARMIES OF A NEW EMPIRE!

The End

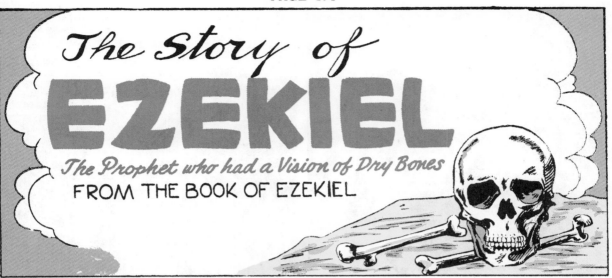

The Story of EZEKIEL

The Prophet who had a Vision of Dry Bones

FROM THE BOOK OF EZEKIEL

WHEN JERUSALEM FELL AND THE ISRAELITES WERE CAPTURED, KING NEBUCHADNEZZAR COMMANDED THAT THEY BE TAKEN TO BABYLON ---

KING NEBUCHADNEZZAR ALLOWS US JEWS TO SETTLE IN COLONIES ABOUT BABYLON!

SOME OF US ARE CONTENT WITH OUR NEW HOMES

BUT WILL WE BE FREE?

OTHERS WEREN'T HAPPY

WE REMEMBER ZION.!

HOW CAN WE SING IN A STRANGE LAND?

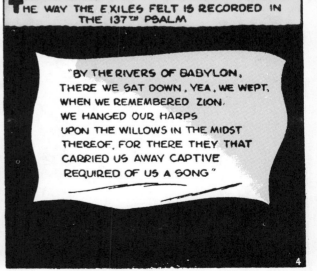

THE WAY THE EXILES FELT IS RECORDED IN THE 137TH PSALM

"BY THE RIVERS OF BABYLON, THERE WE SAT DOWN, YEA, WE WEPT, WHEN WE REMEMBERED ZION. WE HANGED OUR HARPS UPON THE WILLOWS IN THE MIDST THEREOF, FOR THERE THEY THAT CARRIED US AWAY CAPTIVE REQUIRED OF US A SONG"

ISRAELITES ARE BREAKING GOD'S LAWS IN JERUSALEM AND HERE IN BABYLON. I WARN THEM, EZEKIEL ---

YES, A VISION FROM GOD! BUT I BELIEVE THAT WHEN ISRAEL IS REUNITED, THE PEOPLE WILL REPENT AND WILL BE REDEEMED!

EZEKIEL HAD ANOTHER DREAM ABOUT A VALLEY OF BONES

DRY BONES LYING ON THE SAND!

CAN THESE BONES LIVE?

GOD, ONLY YOU KNOW!

I WILL MAKE THESE BONES LIVE --

ANYTHING IS POSSIBLE FOR YOU, GOD!

AS EZEKIEL WATCHES, IN HIS DREAM, THE BONES TURN INTO PEOPLE ''''

THEY ARE PEOPLE —BUT THEY BREATHE NOT! CAN THEY LIVE?

EZEKIEL TALKED TO THE EXILED PEOPLE OF ISRAEL AND TOLD THEM OF HIS WONDERFUL VISIONS ―――

AND I SAW THE TEMPLE OF JERUSALEM BEING REBUILT AGAIN...

"AND FROM UNDER THE DOOR CAME A BEAUTIFUL STREAM. AND EVERYWHERE THESE WATERS WENT THEY TOOK HEALING WITH THEM.....

THIS USED TO BE THE DEAD SEA. NO FISH COULD LIVE IN IT, BUT NOW THERE ARE MANY FISH. EVERYTHING LIVES WHEREVER THE RIVER COMES!

"AND ON THE BANK OF THIS WONDERFUL RIVER GREW TREES WHOSE LEAVES NEVER WITHERED, AND WHOSE FRUIT WAS SO ABUNDANT IT COULD NEVER BE USED UP. THE FRUIT SHALL BE OUR FOOD, AND THE LEAVES OUR MEDICINE."

BUT WHAT CAN THAT VISION MEAN, MASTER?

THE TEMPLE IS OUR FAITH IN RIGHTEOUSNESS. THE RIVER THAT FLOWS OUT OF THE TEMPLE IS THE TRUTH WHICH BRINGS LIFE AND HEALING TO ALL THE NATIONS OF THE EARTH. THE FRUIT IS THE FRUIT OF TRUTH AND WILL NOURISH US!

BUT THE TEMPLE MUST BE PURIFIED, AND OUR LIVES MUST BE GOOD IN EVERY WAY, OR THE RIVER WILL DRY UP!

EZEKIEL DIED IN THE LAND OF EXILE, BUT MEN REMEMBERED HIS TEACHINGS, AND AFTER MANY YEARS HIS FELLOW-COUNTRYMEN WERE FREED FROM THE BABYLONIANS, AND WENT BACK TO REBUILD THE HOLY TEMPLE OF JERUSALEM, AS EZEKIEL HAD DREAMED IN HIS VISION.

The Story of NEHEMIAH
The Rebuilder of the Jerusalem Wall

FROM THE BOOK OF NEHEMIAH

THE PROUD CITY OF JERUSALEM HAD STOOD THROUGH MANY WARS, BUT NEBUCHADNEZZAR AND HIS HOSTS FROM BABYLON FINALLY CONQUERED IT AFTER THREE YEARS OF SIEGE ~

NEBUCHADNEZZAR HAS WON A GREAT VICTORY!

WE BABYLONIANS WILL RAZE JERUSALEM TO THE GROUND, AND CARRY THE PEOPLE OFF AS OUR SLAVES!

SO THE HEBREWS BECAME STRANGERS IN STRANGE LANDS. MANY SETTLED IN BABYLON, BUT THEY NEVER FORGOT THEIR HOMELAND~

IT'S BEAUTIFUL HERE, BUT IT'S NOT LIKE HOME!

I AM SO HOMESICK FOR OUR LAND OF ZION!

SING ONE OF OUR HEBREW SONGS!

LISTEN, THEN—

BY THE RIVERS OF BABYLON, THERE WE SAT DOWN. YEA, WE WEPT, WHEN WE REMEMBERED ZION. IF I FORGET THEE, O JERUSALEM, LET MY RIGHT HAND FORGET HER CUNNING. IF I DO NOT REMEMBER THEE, LET MY TONGUE CLEAVE TO THE ROOF OF MY MOUTH; IF I PREFER NOT JERUSALEM ABOVE MY CHIEF JOY!

NEBUCHADNEZZAR, THE CONQUEROR, WAS AT LAST CONQUERED BY CYRUS, EMPEROR OF THE MEDES AND THE PERSIANS. CYRUS WAS FRIENDLY TO THE CHILDREN OF ISRAEL ~

YOU CHILDREN OF ISRAEL WHO WERE CARRIED INTO CAPTIVITY SHALL GO BACK TO YOUR COUNTRY AND BUILD YOUR TEMPLE AGAIN!

SO 42,360 MEN, WOMEN AND CHILDREN IN ALL, RETURNED TO THE RUINED CITY OF JERUSALEM ~

WE WILL REBUILD OUR TEMPLE, AND OUR CITY!

OUR NATION WILL BE GREAT AGAIN!

BUT ENEMIES TOLD CYRUS THAT THE CHILDREN OF ISRAEL WERE PLOTTING AGAINST HIM~

OUR ENEMIES TOLD THE KING WE PLAN TO REBEL!

CONSPIRATORS!

NOW THE KING HAS DECREED WE MUST STOP BUILDING THE TEMPLE!

THROUGH LONG YEARS, AS KING FOLLOWED KING, THE CHILDREN OF ISRAEL SOUGHT IN VAIN FOR PERMISSION TO REBUILD THEIR BEAUTIFUL TEMPLE, AT LAST A NEW KING, ARTAXERXES, CAME TO THE THRONE---

JERUSALEM WAS A REBELLIOUS CITY. IF YOU LET THE PEOPLE REBUILD THE TEMPLE, THEY WILL NOT PAY TRIBUTE TO YOU ANY LONGER!

THEN I FORBID THEM TO REBUILD IT!

ARTAXERXES' CUP-BEARER WAS A MAN NAMED NEHEMIAH, DESCENDANT OF ONE OF THE EXILED FAMILIES FROM JERUSALEM---

I LIKE TO HAVE YOU AROUND ME, NEHEMIAH-- YOU'RE SO CHEERFUL!

THANK YOU, SIRE!

ONE DAY, NEHEMIAH HAD SOME VISITORS---

MY BROTHER, HANANI! WELCOME!

I HAVE COME FROM JERUSALEM TO VISIT YOU, AND THESE ARE MY FRIENDS!

UNTIL LATE THAT NIGHT, NEHEMIAH AND HIS GUESTS TALKED OF THEIR HOMELAND~

AND IS JERUSALEM STILL IN RUINS?

IF YOU COULD SEE WHAT A WRECK OUR CITY IS, YOU WOULD WEEP, NEHEMIAH!

AND NEHEMIAH PRAYED-----

MY PEOPLE HAVE SINNED AGAINST YOU, LORD, AND YOU HAVE SAID, I WILL SCATTER THEM ABROAD AMONG THE NATIONS. BUT IF WE KEEP YOUR COMMANDMENTS, YOU HAVE SAID, YOU WOULD GATHER US TOGETHER AND BRING US BACK AGAIN TO OUR OLD HOME! OH, HEAR MY PRAYER, LORD!

YOU ARE NOT SICK, NEHEMIAH-- WHY ARE YOU SO SAD, THEN?

WHY SHOULD I NOT BE SAD, SIRE, WHEN THE CITY OF MY FATHERS LIES IN RUINS!

O KING, SEND ME TO JERUSALEM AND LET ME REBUILD THE CITY WALL!

VERY WELL. ONCE I FORBADE YOUR PEOPLE TO REBUILD LEST THEY GROW PROUD AND REBEL-- BUT I TRUST YOU, NEHEMIAH-- YOU MAY GO!

ESCORTED BY THE KING'S HORSEMEN, NEHEMIAH ARRIVES IN JERUSALEM, ENEMIES BEGIN THEIR WORK~

LOOK, TOBIAH, THAT'S NEHEMIAH, HE'S COME TO REBUILD THE WALL. A TROUBLEMAKER!

WE'LL TAKE CARE OF HIM, SANBALLAT!

MEANWHILE, NEHEMIAH CALLED THE PEOPLE OF JERUSALEM TOGETHER~

SEE HOW JERUSALEM, THE CITY OF YOUR FATHERS, LIES WASTE! LET US REBUILD THE WALL OF JERUSALEM!

WE'LL DO IT!

WE'LL ALL WORK!

SANBALLAT AND TOBIAH MOCK NEHEMIAH'S EFFORTS~

HO! SO YOU'RE REBUILDING THE WALL? REBELLING AGAINST THE KING, THAT'S MORE LIKE IT!

CALL THAT A WALL? A FOX COULD KNOCK IT OVER

YOU HAVE NO RIGHT HERE!

DAY AFTER DAY THE WALL ROSE~

YOU'RE WORKING WELL! NOTHING CAN STOP YOU!

NOW SANBALLAT AND TOBIAH MADE A PLOT URGING THE HOSTILE TRIBESMEN AROUND JERUSALEM TO ATTACK NEHEMIAH AND HIS WORKERS~

NEHEMIAH IS YOUR ENEMY!

HE MAY ATTACK YOU! ATTACK HIM FIRST!

WE'LL RAID JERUSALEM AND TEAR DOWN HIS WALL!

A MESSENGER TELLS NEHEMIAH~

THE TRIBES ARE MASSING TO ATTACK US. SANBALLAT PUT THEM UP TO IT!

HALF OF OUR MEN MUST ARM THEMSELVES WITH SWORDS AND SPEARS—THEY WILL GUARD THE WALL WHILE THE REST OF US WORK!

DON'T BE AFRAID OF THEM! FIGHT FOR YOUR SONS AND DAUGHTERS, YOUR WIVES AND YOUR HOMES!

DAY AND NIGHT WE'LL GUARD AND WORK!

KNOWING THE HEBREWS WERE READY, THE TRIBESMEN NEVER ATTACKED, AND WORK WENT FORWARD ON THE WALL~

NOW CAME MORE TROUBLE- THIS TIME FROM WITHIN JERUSALEM~

WHILE WE WORK ON THE WALL, WE CANNOT FARM OUR LAND!

WE MUST BORROW FROM THE RICH TO PAY OUR TAXES!

WHEN WE CAN'T REPAY THEY TAKE OUR FARMS AND VINEYARDS!

NEHEMIAH FACES THE RICH MONEY LENDERS~

WHAT YOU'RE DOING IS BAD! THESE MEN ARE YOUR BROTHERS! GIVE THEM BACK THEIR FARMS AND VINEYARDS!

WE WILL DO AS YOU SAY, NEHEMIAH!

THEIR OTHER PLOTS HAVING FAILED SANBALLAT AND TOBIAH HATCH NEW SCHEMES TO WRECK NEHEMIAH'S WORK~

DON'T GO, NEHEMIAH! IT'S A PLAN TO CATCH YOU!

We are your friends. Let us meet together on the Plain of Ono! Sanballat and Tobiah

TELL SANBALLAT AND TOBIAH THAT I AM DOING A GREAT WORK AND I CANNOT COME!

BUT THE MESSENGER COMES BACK~

WHAT, ARE YOU HERE AGAIN? FOUR TIMES I'VE SAID NO! WHAT NOW?

READ IT, NEHEMIAH!

We know why you are building the wall. You want to rebel, and make yourself King, but we will tell King Artaxerxes! You had better come and meet

NEHEMIAH WRITES AN ANSWER~

I WILL WRITE "WHAT YOU SAY IS NOT TRUE. I DO NOT SEEK TO BE KING OF THE HEBREWS YOU ARE MAKING UP THESE STORIES!"

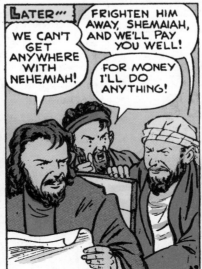

LATER~

WE CAN'T GET ANYWHERE WITH NEHEMIAH!

FRIGHTEN HIM AWAY, SHEMAIAH, AND WE'LL PAY YOU WELL!

FOR MONEY I'LL DO ANYTHING!

LATER IN NEHEMIAH'S HOUSE~

I'M WARNING YOU AS A FRIEND, NEHEMIAH! HIDE IN THE HEATHEN TEMPLE! THEY ARE OUT TO KILL YOU!

THAT WOULD BE WICKED! NO, I MUST STAY AND BUILD THE WALL-I'M NOT AFRAID!

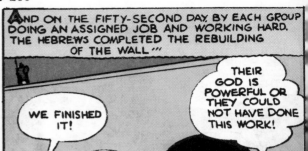

BUT WE PAID YOU TO FRIGHTEN HIM AWAY!

HE IS FEARLESS! HE WILL NOT BE FRIGHTENED.

AND ON THE FIFTY-SECOND DAY, BY EACH GROUP DOING AN ASSIGNED JOB AND WORKING HARD, THE HEBREWS COMPLETED THE REBUILDING OF THE WALL ⋯

WE FINISHED IT!

PRAISE GOD!

THEIR GOD IS POWERFUL OR THEY COULD NOT HAVE DONE THIS WORK!

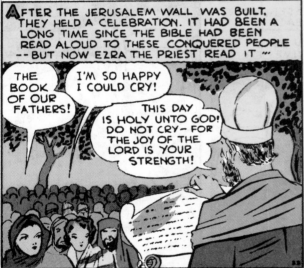

AFTER THE JERUSALEM WALL WAS BUILT, THEY HELD A CELEBRATION. IT HAD BEEN A LONG TIME SINCE THE BIBLE HAD BEEN READ ALOUD TO THESE CONQUERED PEOPLE -- BUT NOW EZRA THE PRIEST READ IT ⋯

THE BOOK OF OUR FATHERS!

I'M SO HAPPY I COULD CRY!

THIS DAY IS HOLY UNTO GOD! DO NOT CRY— FOR THE JOY OF THE LORD IS YOUR STRENGTH!

5. THE BUILDERS SIGNED A COVENANT TO KEEP THE FAITH AND WORSHIP THEIR LORD AND OBEY THE LAWS OF GOD!

THE WALL WAS DEDICATED WITH SINGING AND WITH HARP PLAYING ⋯

♪ THOU, EVEN THOU, ART LORD ALONE — ♪ THOU HAST MADE HEAVEN, THE EARTH AND ALL THINGS THAT ARE THEREIN, THE SEAS, AND ALL THAT IS THEREIN, AND THE HOST OF HEAVEN WORSHIPPETH THEE ♪

NOW THAT HIS WORK WAS DONE, NEHEMIAH KNEW HE MUST RETURN TO KING ARTAXERXES AGAIN ⋯

YOU HAVE DONE MUCH FOR YOUR PEOPLE, NEHEMIAH!

I PROMISED THE KING I WOULD RETURN, AND I MUST GO. BUT I WILL NOT FORGET YOU, AND I WILL COME AGAIN!

So Nehemiah lived in Persia for twelve years - then he returned to Jerusalem

DO YOU SEE MANY CHANGES, NEHEMIAH?

YES, AND FOR THE WORSE! GREED EVERYWHERE - ON THE SABBATH MEN THINK ONLY OF MAKING MONEY!

Nehemiah instructs the gatekeeper~

SHUT THE GATES ON THE SABBATH DAY. LET THESE GREEDY ONES STAY OUTSIDE!

Nehemiah finds desecration in the temple

WHAT'S THIS, ELIASHIB? YOU'RE PROFANING THE TEMPLE! GET OUT - AND STAY OUT!

He then warns the people ~~~

YOUR FATHERS DID EVIL AND BROUGHT ALL THIS TROUBLE ON US! DO YOU WANT TO DO THE SAME?

WE WILL DO WHAT IS RIGHT, NEHEMIAH!

NO! NO!

So, NEHEMIAH REFORMED THE EVILS THAT HAD ARISEN AMONG HIS PEOPLE AND BROUGHT THEM TO OBEY THE LAWS OF GOD

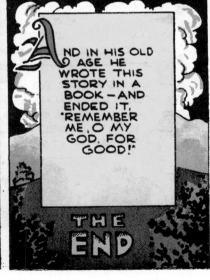

And in his old age he wrote this story in a book - and ended it, "REMEMBER ME, O MY GOD, FOR GOOD!"

THE END

THE STORY OF DANIEL

PART ONE

ARRANGED FROM THE OLD TESTAMENT BOOK OF DANIEL

MENE, MENE, TEKEL, UPHARSIN.

GOD HATH NUMBERED THY KINGDOM AND FINISHED IT.

THOU ART WEIGHED IN THE BALANCES, AND ART FOUND WANTING

THY KINGDOM IS DIVIDED, AND GIVEN TO THE MEDES AND PERSIANS.

NEBUCHADNEZZAR, KING OF THE CHALDEANS, OVERTHREW JERUSALEM AND TOOK THE CAPTIVES, INCLUDING DANIEL AND HIS THREE COMPANIONS, BACK TO BABYLON ----

GATHER THE HANDSOMEST, HEALTHIEST AND MOST INTELLIGENT ISRAELITE BOYS AND GIVE THEM THREE YEARS OF TRAINING IN OUR LANGUAGE AND CUSTOMS!

YES, MASTER, THEY SHALL BE TRAINED!

DANIEL AND HIS THREE FRIENDS WERE AMONG THOSE CHOSEN - THEY SOON DREW THE ATTENTION OF THEIR TEACHER ---

WE START TRAINING WITH NEW NAMES — I, DANIEL, AM CALLED BELTESHAZZAR

WE ARE FAVORED AT THE KING'S COURT!

YOU MUST LEARN **OUR** WAYS OF EATING AND DRINKING, AND GET USED TO YOUR NEW NAMES!

WE HAVE STARTED BY ACCEPTING NEW NAMES — I, HANANIAH, AM SHADRACH, MISHAEL IS NOW MESHACH!

I AZARIAH BECAME ABED-NEGO!

DANIEL RESOLVED IN HIS HEART THAT HE WOULD NOT DEFILE HIMSELF BY EATING THE KING'S RICH FOOD AND DRINKING HIS WINE ---

GIVE PLAIN FOOD AND WATER TO US FOUR BOYS FOR TEN DAYS — THEN SEE IF WE ARE NOT IN BETTER CONDITION THAN THE OTHERS!

I'LL DO IT, BUT I MAY LOSE MY HEAD FOR DISOBEYING THE KING'S ORDERS!

THE LADS DID SO WELL ON PLAIN FOOD, THAT IT WAS CONTINUED THROUGHOUT THE THREE YEARS ~~~

THESE ARE THE FOUR BOYS WE HAVE SPOKEN OF, MASTER!

LET ME QUESTION THEM!

THE YOUTHS REPLIED TO ALL QUESTIONS AND SHOWED THEMSELVES CLEVER, WHICH PLEASED NEBUCHADNEZZAR ~~~

IN ALL MATTERS OF WISDOM AND UNDERSTANDING YOU AND YOUR COMPANIONS ARE TEN TIMES BETTER THAN MY WISE MEN!

NOT LONG AFTERWARD, NEBUCHADNEZZAR HAD DREAMS THAT TERRIFIED HIM SO HE COULD NOT SLEEP ~~~

WHAT IS THE MATTER WITH ME? ~ I CAN'T SLEEP, THINKING OF MY DREAMS!

CALL MY ASTROLOGERS, MY SORCERERS, ALL MY WISE MEN TO ME! ~ I MUST ASK THEM TO EXPLAIN MY DREAMS!

YES, O KING!

WHAT IS THIS DREAM I HAD? ~ I CAN'T REMEMBER IT!

YOU MUST TELL US THE DREAM, O KING, SO WE CAN INTERPRET IT!

YOU FOOLS! YOU SHOULD KNOW THE DREAM AS WELL AS THE INTERPRETATION ~ TELL IT OR YOU DIE!

BUT, MASTER, WHAT YOU ASK IS BEYOND ANY MAN ~ WE CANNOT REPLY UNTIL YOU TELL US THE DREAM!

PAGE 204

Daniel speaks with the King's head guardsman—

WHAT ARE YOU SO EXCITED ABOUT, ARIOCH?

BAD NEWS! THE WISE MEN CAN'T TELL THE DREAM THE KING HAS FORGOTTEN—HE THREATENS TO KILL ALL OF THEM, WHICH INCLUDES YOU AND YOUR FRIENDS!

TAKE ME BEFORE THE KING— PERHAPS I CAN INTERPRET THE DREAM!

WHAT NOW?— IS THIS ONE OF THE ISRAELITES?

OH, MASTER, IT IS BELTESHAZZAR— HE SAYS HE MAY INTERPRET YOUR DREAMS!

GIVE ME A LITTLE TIME, SIRE, SPARE THE WISE MEN AND I SHALL FIND YOUR ANSWERS— I SHALL TELL AND INTERPRET YOUR FORGOTTEN DREAM!

I AGREE, BUT NOT TOO LONG, ISRAELITE!

In the meantime, Daniel requests his friends to pray that God give him the secret of the dream—

I THANK YOU, GOD, FOR REVEALING THE SECRET TO ME IN A DREAM—I SHALL GO TO NEBUCHADNEZZAR IN THE MORNING!

YOUR DREAM, O KING, WAS OF A VAST STATUE OF GOLD AND SILVER AND BRASS AND CLAY! —AND A GREAT ROCK SMASHED IT, BREAKING IT IN PARTS— THEN THE ROCK GREW INTO A MOUNTAIN!

RIGHT—THAT IS THE DREAM!

NEITHER YOUR WISE MEN NOR ANY MAN CAN REVEAL SUCH THINGS—IT IS ONLY GOD IN HEAVEN, THE TRUE GOD WHOM I WORSHIP, WHO REVEALED THE DREAM TO ME!

NOW FOR THE MEANING OF THE DREAM, BELTESHAZZAR!

O KING, THE IMAGE REPRESENTS THE KINGDOMS OF THE WORLD, AND THOSE TO COME—THE GOLD HEAD REPRESENTS YOU, THE GREATEST OF ALL KINGS!—BUT THE GREAT STONE WRECKS THE IMAGE, AND GROWS TO A MOUNTAIN—SO WILL KINGDOMS FALL—ONE KINGDOM SET UP BY GOD WILL SURVIVE!

YOU ARE TRULY WISE FOR A YOUTH!—FOR YOUR WISDOM I SHALL MAKE YOU GOVERNOR OVER THE PROVINCE OF BABYLON ANSWERING ONLY TO ME FOR YOUR ACTS!

WHILE DANIEL WAS SECOND ONLY TO THE KING AND GIVEN GIFTS, HIS THREE FRIENDS WERE MADE SUBORDINATE RULERS—

I SHALL MAKE SHADRACH, MESHACH AND ABED-NEGO RULERS UNDER ME!

ALTHOUGH THE KING RECOGNIZED DANIEL'S GOD AS THE REVEALER OF DREAMS, HE SET UP AN IMAGE OF GOLD IN THE VALLEY OF DURA ---

THE KING COMMANDS ALL IN BABYLON TO WORSHIP THIS IMAGE!

AND EVERY OFFICER MUST COME TO THE DEDICATION AT ONCE!

WHEN THE MUSICAL INSTRUMENTS PLAY, EVERYONE IS TO FALL DOWN AND WORSHIP MY GOLDEN GOD! THOSE WHO DO NOT, WILL BE THROWN INTO THE FIERY FURNACE AND BURNED TO DEATH!

SHADRACH, MESHACH AND ABED-NEGO REFUSED TO OBEY AND SO THEY WERE ACCUSED OF DEFYING BABYLON'S KING ~~~

WE ACCUSE CERTAIN HEBREWS AND SHALL POINT THEM OUT!-THEY REFUSE TO WORSHIP NEBUCHADNEZZAR'S GOD!

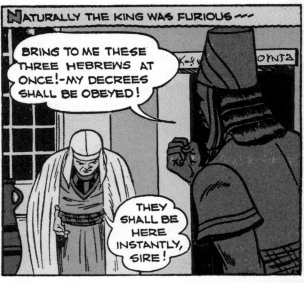

NATURALLY THE KING WAS FURIOUS ~~~

BRING TO ME THESE THREE HEBREWS AT ONCE!-MY DECREES SHALL BE OBEYED!

THEY SHALL BE HERE INSTANTLY, SIRE!

IS IT THEN TRUE THAT YOU WILL NOT BOW DOWN TO THE IMAGE OF MY GOD?

WE SERVE ONLY OUR GOD, WHO WILL DELIVER US-WE WILL NOT SERVE YOUR GODS!

IF WE SUFFER, WE SUFFER. WE SHALL WORSHIP ONLY THE TRUE GOD!

THROW THESE YOUTHS INTO THE FIERY FURNACE-MAKE IT SEVEN TIMES HOTTER!

AT THE KING'S ORDERS, HIS MEN BOUND THE THREE ISRAELITES WITH ALL THEIR CLOTHES ON AND THREW THEM INTO THE FURNACE, AND WERE THEMSELVES KILLED BY THE INTENSE HEAT ~~~

I CAN'T STAND IT-I'M DYING!

THIS TERRIFIC HEAT-WE PERISH!

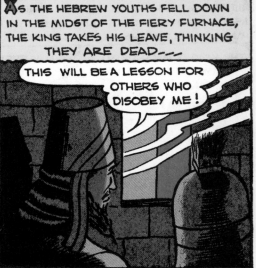

AS THE HEBREW YOUTHS FELL DOWN IN THE MIDST OF THE FIERY FURNACE, THE KING TAKES HIS LEAVE, THINKING THEY ARE DEAD ~~~

THIS WILL BE A LESSON FOR OTHERS WHO DISOBEY ME!

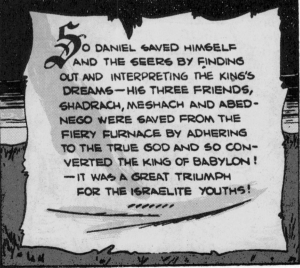

AFTER MANY YEARS, BELSHAZZAR, THE SON OF NEBUCHADNEZZAR, BECAME KING— HE LOVED PLEASURE ONLY～～

LET'S MAKE MERRY, FOR WHO KNOWS, TOMORROW WE MAY DIE!— BRING IN THE SACRED GOLDEN VESSELS TAKEN FROM JERUSALEM!

I, BELSHAZZAR, THE SON OF NEBUCHADNEZZAR, AM RICH AND GREAT—NONE CAN SAY WHAT I SHALL DO!

SUDDENLY, AS THE KING LIFTED A GOLDEN VESSEL, A STRANGE HAND APPEARED ON THE WALL, AND WAS WRITING～～

IT IS IN A STRANGE TONGUE, I CAN'T READ IT!

IT SPELLS DOOM!

MENE, MENE, TEKEL, UPHARSIN

DANIEL IS CALLED TO INTERPRET IT～～

O KING, THAT IS A SIGN AND YOU SURELY SHALL FALL NOW, QUICKER THAN YOUR FATHER DID— FOR YOU HAVE DEFILED THE HOLY VESSELS AND DEFIED OUR GOD!

WHO IS STRONGER THAN I AM?

GOD, SIRE! THE MEDES AND PERSIANS ARE EVEN NOW COMING TO SEIZE BABYLON!

AND SO IT WAS—DANIEL SPOKE ARIGHT～～

IT HAS HAPPENED!—KING BELSHAZZAR IS SLAIN AND DANIEL THE ISRAELITE IS PROCLAIMED RULER—BUT THE PERSIANS AND MEDES ARE CONQUERING US ALL!

THE STORY OF
DANIEL
PART TWO
FROM THE BOOK OF DANIEL

KING DARIUS, HEADING THE MEDES AND PERSIANS, CONQUERS BABYLON IN A SWIFT SIEGE ~~~

AND WHEN DARIUS SAT IN THE KING'S PALACE HE MADE DECREES ~~~

OVER THE PROVINCES OF MY EMPIRE NOW ESTABLISHED, I SHALL PLACE 120 PRINCES — THERE IS ONE HERE WHO SHALL BE MADE FIRST!

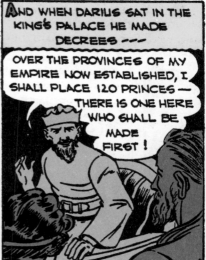

YEA! — THERE SHALL BE OVERLORDS OVER THE PRINCES — DANIEL SHALL BE THE FIRST AND SHALL SERVE UNDER ME!

NOW WHEN THE OFFICIALS WERE APPOINTED, THE NEW PROVINCIAL RULERS WERE JEALOUS OF DANIEL ~~~

LET'S FIND SOMETHING WRONG AND REPORT HIM TO THE KING!

WHAT CAN WE SAY? — HE SEEMS TO HAVE NO FAULTS!

OUR ONLY CHANCE IS TO TRIP HIM IN THE FAITHFUL WORSHIP OF HIS GOD — LET'S HAVE THE KING SIGN A DECREE FOR THE PEOPLE TO WORSHIP ONLY DARIUS!

WE SUGGEST A DECREE, O KING, THAT FOR THIRTY DAYS NO ONE IS TO PRAY TO ANY GOD OR MAN EXCEPT YOU—SHOULD ANYONE DISOBEY, THEN CAST HIM INTO THE DEN OF LIONS!

— I WILL SIGN, FOR I AM SUPREME ON EARTH!

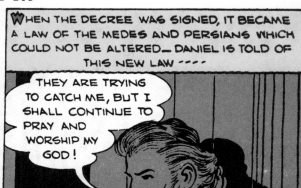

WHEN THE DECREE WAS SIGNED, IT BECAME A LAW OF THE MEDES AND PERSIANS WHICH COULD NOT BE ALTERED— DANIEL IS TOLD OF THIS NEW LAW ----

THEY ARE TRYING TO CATCH ME, BUT I SHALL CONTINUE TO PRAY AND WORSHIP MY GOD!

SO DANIEL IN HIS ROOM CONTINUED TO KNEEL AND PRAY THREE TIMES EACH DAY WITH HIS WINDOWS OPEN TOWARD JERUSALEM, HIS CHILDHOOD HOME ---

O, GOD, STRENGTHEN ME AND KEEP ME TRUE TO MY PROMISE TO WORSHIP ONLY THEE!

LOOK!

DANIEL DOES NOT OBEY THE DECREE OF THE GREAT KING!

NOW HE IS TRAPPED!

DARIUS, SORRY FOR THE DECREE WHICH HE HAD BEEN TRICKED INTO SIGNING, HOPED IN SOME WAY TO SAVE DANIEL ---

ARE YOU SURE THAT DANIEL WAS PRAYING TO HIS GOD?—BRING HIM TO ME!

THE PUNISHMENT, O MIGHTY KING, IS THE DEN OF LIONS!

THE KING COMMANDS YOU TO APPEAR AT ONCE, DANIEL! —COME!

I SUPPOSE YOU ARE SATISFIED NOW TO HAVE YOUR EVIL PLANS WORKING OUT!

DANIEL'S ACCUSERS REMINDED THE KING OF HIS DECREE TO PUNISH VIOLATORS ---

THE LAW MUST BE OBEYED, BUT YOUR GOD WHOM YOU TRUST WILL DELIVER YOU!

I WILL OBEY GOD NO MATTER WHAT HAPPENS!

INTO THE DEN YOU GO!

THE GREAT KING COMES AND WILL CLOSE THE OPENING WITH A LARGE STONE AND SEAL IT WITH HIS SIGNET RING!

NO ONE MAY OPEN THIS BUT MYSELF — I SEAL THE DEN WITH MY OWN SEAL — DANIEL WILL BE KILLED!

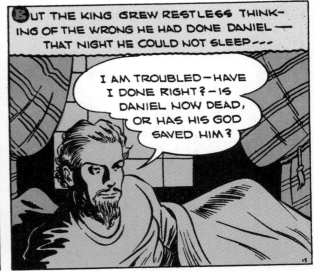

BUT THE KING GREW RESTLESS THINKING OF THE WRONG HE HAD DONE DANIEL — THAT NIGHT HE COULD NOT SLEEP ---

I AM TROUBLED — HAVE I DONE RIGHT? — IS DANIEL NOW DEAD, OR HAS HIS GOD SAVED HIM?

BUT DANIEL WAS NOT DEAD — THE WILD LIONS HAD NOT HARMED HIM SINCE GOD SENT HIS ANGEL TO PROTECT HIM ---

EARLY NEXT MORNING DARIUS HASTENS TO THE LION'S DEN~~~

DANIEL, HAS YOUR GOD BEEN ABLE TO DELIVER YOU?

O KING, LIVE FOREVER — MY GOD HAS SENT HIS ANGEL, AND HAS SHUT THE LIONS' MOUTHS, THAT THEY HAVE NOT HURT ME!

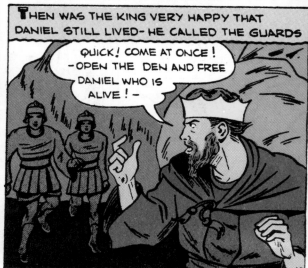

THEN WAS THE KING VERY HAPPY THAT DANIEL STILL LIVED- HE CALLED THE GUARDS

QUICK! COME AT ONCE! -OPEN THE DEN AND FREE DANIEL WHO IS ALIVE! -

HURRY, HURRY, MEN!

ALL TOGETHER NOW AND WE WILL HAVE IT OPEN!

MY LORD GOD SAVED ME, SIRE!

I AM GLAD YOU ARE SAFE - THOSE JEALOUS MEN TRICKED ME INTO SIGNING THAT DECREE — NOW I WILL CAST THEM INTO THE LIONS' DEN!

THE WICKED PLOTTERS WERE PUT TO DEATH — KING DARIUS ACCEPTED DANIEL'S GOD AND COMMANDED THE PEOPLE TO ACCEPT HIM ALSO—

I AND MY PEOPLE WILL NOW WORSHIP YOUR GOD! COME SERVE ME AS BEFORE!

YOU ARE A WISE KING TO RECOGNIZE THE LIVING GOD — I WILL SERVE YOU FAITHFULLY IN MY RESTORED POSITION!

IN THE DAYS THAT FOLLOWED, DANIEL HAD MANY PROPHETIC DREAMS—HE OFTEN FASTED AND PRAYED TO GOD WEARING SACKCLOTH—

GOD OF MY FATHERS, GREAT AND POWERFUL GOD WHOM I LOVE, HEAR MY VOICE FOR I KNOW THAT TROUBLESOME TIMES ARE AHEAD!

SO DANIEL ASKS A FAVOR OF HIS GOD—

LET YOUR ANGER CEASE AGAINST JERUSALEM AND MY PEOPLE!—LET JERUSALEM, WHICH WAS WRECKED IN THE PERSIAN CONQUEST, BE RESTORED!

SUDDENLY—

I HAVE COME TO GIVE YOU UNDERSTANDING, DANIEL!

AT THE END OF SEVENTY WEEKS THERE SHALL COME EVENTS AND JERUSALEM SHALL BE RESTORED BY THE PERSIANS— —IN THAT TIME YOU AND YOUR PEOPLE SHALL CONFESS YOUR SINS AND REPENT!

IT IS THE ANGEL GABRIEL!

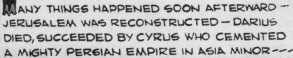

MANY THINGS HAPPENED SOON AFTERWARD — JERUSALEM WAS RECONSTRUCTED — DARIUS DIED, SUCCEEDED BY CYRUS WHO CEMENTED A MIGHTY PERSIAN EMPIRE IN ASIA MINOR ---

ONE DAY DANIEL WALKS BY THE BANKS OF THE RIVER HIDDEKEL AND SEES A VISION, BUT THOSE WITH HIM SEE IT NOT ---

THE MEN SAW NOT THE VISION — BUT A GREAT FEAR FELL UPON THEM, SO THAT THEY FLED TO HIDE THEMSELVES ---

THE GROUND TREMBLES — LET US HIDE!

A VISION IN LINEN WITH A GIRDLE OF GOLD!

I COME TO WARN YOU OF TROUBLES THAT WILL DESCEND — BUT, DANIEL, STAND STEADFAST IN THE WAY OF GOD!

IN TIME THE KING OF GREECE INVADES PERSIA AND UPSETS THE EMPIRE AND A PERIOD OF CHAOS BEGINS ---

THE KING OF GREECE HAS COME WITH HIS LEGIONS!

PERSIA FALLS!

AND CIVIL WARS START, WHILE SECTIONS OF PERSIA SET UP THEIR OWN PETTY RULERS ---

THE NORTH HAS BROKEN FROM THE SOUTH!

THE SOUTH WILL HAVE ITS OWN KING AND CONQUER!

THE GREEKS MARCH IN ---

NONE SHALL STOP US AND WE SHALL RULE ALL THE MEDES AND PERSIANS!

NOT LONG AFTERWARD A NEW INVADER APPEARED —THE ROMANS! — THEY SCATTERED ALL OPPOSITION BEFORE THEM——

WE SHALL RULE THE ENTIRE EARTH! — STRIKE FOR CAESAR AND THE ARMY!

MANY FELL — BURNINGS WERE FREQUENT IN PERSIA AND CONFUSION REIGNED——

WE SHALL BURN THE HOMES OF ALL WHO DEFY THE ROMANS!

SO ROME TOOK PERSIA AND ADDED ASIA MINOR DOWN TO THE BORDERS OF EGYPT——

THE TIMES ARE UPSET AND EVERYTHING IS CRUMBLING, FOR THE OLD ORDER IS BEING WIPED OUT!

THEN THE HEAVENS BURST OPEN AND THE ANGEL MICHAEL APPEARS TO DANIEL——

I AM SENT TO YOU, DANIEL, TO GIVE YOU AN UNDERSTANDING SPIRIT!

THIS TURMOIL SHALL CONTINUE FOR A TIME, EVEN A TIME AND A HALF, BEFORE PEACE COMES AGAIN, DANIEL — MANY SHALL BE TRIED AND TESTED IN THESE UPSET DAYS — BUT YOU MUST ABIDE IN RESTFULNESS AND REMAIN QUIET OF HEART — FOR CONTENTMENT SHALL RETURN AND YOU SHALL SEE A NEW WORLD!

END

The Story of JONAH AND THE WHALE

ARRANGED FROM THE OLD TESTAMENT BOOK OF JONAH~

NOW THE ANCIENT CITY OF NINEVEH WAS VERY WICKED. SO THE LORD COMMANDED JONAH, THE SON OF AMITTAI, TO GO THERE AND PREACH AGAINST THE SINS OF THE CITY~

"ARISE, JONAH, AND GO TO NINEVEH AND GIVE THEM MY MESSAGE TO CEASE THEIR EVIL!"

BUT JONAH DISOBEYS~

I CANNOT DO WHAT THE LORD WANTS ME TO. NO! INSTEAD, I'LL RUN AWAY! I'LL LEAVE THE COUNTRY!

JONAH ARRIVES AT THE SEAPORT OF JOPPA AND FINDS A SHIP~

I'LL ASK WHERE THIS SHIP IS BOUND FOR.

HERE IS MY FARE FOR THE VOYAGE.

GOOD! WE'LL SET SAIL AT ONCE FOR TARSHISH.

SUDDENLY, AS THE SHIP SAILS ON~

GET READY! THIS WIND MEANS A MIGHTY TEMPEST!

EACH SAILOR, AFRAID, CALLED ON HIS GOD TO SAVE HIM~

OH, BAAL, PRESERVE US!

GOD OF THE STORM, BE MERCIFUL!

THROW OVER OUR CARGO AND EXCESS WEIGHT SO THAT THE SHIP WILL FLOAT!!

SO THEY THREW OVER THEIR CARGO. THE STORM DID NOT ABATE~

BUT IN THE BOTTOM OF THE SHIP LIES JONAH, ASLEEP!

WHAT MEANS THIS? YOU SLEEP THROUGH A TEMPEST?

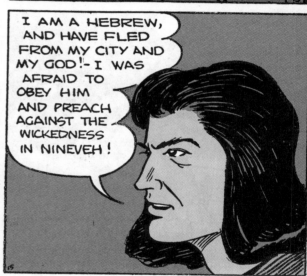